BL
2370
.H5
H57
1991

Hittite myths.

MAY 0 8 1993

$19.95

DATE			

Hittite Myths

Society of Biblical Literature
Writings from the Ancient World

Edited by
Burke O. Long

Volume 2
Hittite Myths
translated by Harry A. Hoffner, Jr.
edited by Gary M. Beckman

Hittite Myths

Translated by
Harry A. Hoffner, Jr.

Edited by
Gary M. Beckman

Scholars Press
Atlanta, Georgia

HITTITE MYTHS
Copyright © 1990
Society of Biblical Literature

The Society of Biblical Literature gratefully acknowledges a grant
from the National Endowment for the Humanities to underwrite
certain editorial and research expenses of the Writings from
the Ancient World series. Published results and interpretations
do not necessarily represent the view of the Endowment.

Library of Congress Cataloging-in-Publication Data

Hittite myths / translated by Harry A. Hoffner, Jr. ; edited by Gary
M. Beckman.
    p.   cm. — (Writings from the ancient world : no. 2)
    Includes bibliographical references.
    ISBN 1-55540-481-2. — ISBN 1-55540-482-0 (pbk.)
    1. Mythology, Hittite. I. Hoffner, Harry A. II. Beckman, Gary
M. III. Series.
BL2370.H5H57   1990   90-36218
299'.199--dc20   CIP

Printed in the United States of America
on acid-free paper

Contents

Editor's Foreword

This book is the first of many in the series Writings from the Ancient World (WAW), which will present up-to-date and felicitous English translations of important documents from the ancient Near East. Covering the period from the beginning of Sumerian civilization to the age of Alexander, WAW provides access to the fullness of major cultural areas of the ancient world. The editors have kept in mind a broad audience that includes, among others, scholars in the humanities for whom convenient access to new and reliable translations will aid comparative work; general readers, educators, and students for whom these materials may help increase awareness of our cultural roots in preclassical civilizations; specialists in particular cultures of the ancient world who may not control the languages of neighboring societies. The series thereby tries to meet research needs while contributing to general education.

The editors envision that over time this series will include collections of myths, epics, poetry, and law codes; historical and diplomatic materials such as treaties and commemorative inscriptions; texts from daily life, including letters and commercial documents. Other volumes will offer translations of hymns, prayers, rituals, and other documents of religious practice. The aim is to provide a representative, rather than exhaustive, sample of writings that broadly represent the cultural remains of various ancient civilizations.

The preparation of this volume was supported in part by a generous grant from the Division of Research Programs of the National Endowment for the Humanities. Significant funding has also been made available by the Society of Biblical Literature. In addition, all those persons involved in preparing this volume have received significant financial and clerical assistance from their respective institutions. Were it not for these expressions of confidence in our intentions, the arduous tasks of preparation, translation, editing, and publication—indeed, planning for the series itself—simply would not have been undertaken.

Burke O. Long

Abbreviations

AA	*Archäologischer Anzeiger*
AJA	*American Journal of Archaeology*
ANET	*Ancient Near Eastern Texts relating to the Old Testament* (ed. J. B. Pritchard; 3d ed. with Suppl.; Princeton: Princeton University Press, 1969)
AnSt	*Anatolian Studies*
AoF	*Altorientalische Forschungen*
ArOr	*Archiv Orientální*
BASOR	*Bulletin of the American Schools of Oriental Research*
CHD	*The Hittite Dictionary of the Oriental Institute of the University of Chicago*
CTH	*Catalogue des textes hittites* (Laroche 1971)
JANES	*Journal of the Ancient Near Eastern Society*
JNES	*Journal of Near Eastern Studies*
JRAS	*Journal of the Royal Asiatic Society*
KBo	*Keilschrifttexte aus Boghazköi*
KUB	*Keilschrifturkunden aus Boghazköi*
MIO	*Mitteilungen des Institut für Orientforschung*
OA	*Oriens Antiquus*
OLZ	*Orientalistische Literaturzeitung*
Or	*Orientalia*
RHA	*Revue hittite et asianique*
RhM	*Rheinisches Museum für Philologie*
SMEA	*Studi Micenei ed Egeo-Anatolici*
UF	*Ugarit-Forschungen*
VBoT	*Verstreute Boghazköi-Texte*
VO	*Vicino Oriente*
ZA	*Zeitschrift für Assyriologie*
ZDMG	*Zeitschrift der Deutschen Morgenländischen Gesellschaft*

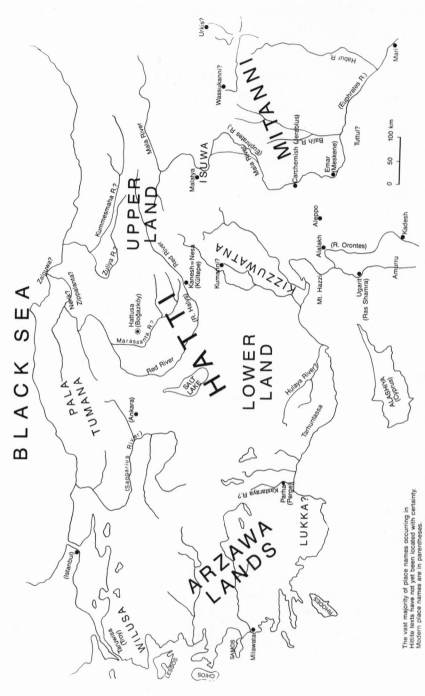

The vast majority of place names occurring in
Hittite texts have not yet been located with certainty.
Modern place names are in parentheses.

Explanation of Signs

Single brackets [ ] enclose restorations.

Angle brackets ‹ › enclose words omitted by the original scribe.

Parentheses ( ) enclose additions in the English translation.

A row of dots . . . indicates gaps in the text or untranslatable words.

Introduction

The key to understanding any society is its living context. No amount of research into the events that transpired during its history, examination of its material remains, or analysis of its language can substitute for the intuitive understanding which comes from being a part of that era and society. Obviously, it is impossible for us to have this experience for any society of the past. But this *caveat* need not discourage us from attempting with realistic, limited expectations to understand Hittite civilization from its artifacts, and especially its writings.

Since the middle of the nineteenth century, Western explorers have been fascinated by the remains of those long-dead civilizations which once flowered in the lands bordering the eastern end of the Mediterranean basin and the territories immediately to the east. Above-ground Hittite remains — though not at the time recognized as Hittite — were sketched by Charles Texier as early as 1839. Hieroglyphic monuments, which are now known to be written in the Luwian language, drew the attention of J. L. Burckhardt in 1812 and William Wright and Archibald Sayce in the 1870s. But scientific interest in the people now called the Hittites first burgeoned after Hugo Winckler and Theodor Makridi began their excavation of a huge site near the Turkish village of Boghazköy in 1906. They soon learned that this was the location of the Hittite capital, Hattusa. Royal archives found in storerooms on the eastern side of the Great Temple in the Lower City and others located in Building A on the acropolis yielded about ten thousand clay tablets inscribed with the familiar cuneiform script. Most were written in an unintelligible language, correctly judged to be the native language, Hittite. Others, written in Babylonian, the diplomatic *lingua franca* of that time, could be read immediately. These provided enough information to confirm the identification of the site and the dates of its occupation. The Hittite language itself was deciphered in 1915 by Bedrich Hrozný, a professor of Assyriology at the University of Vienna. Since the values of the cuneiform signs were well known from Akkadian, this "decipherment" consisted of the identification of the grammatical structure of the language, which was discovered to be Indo-European, in many respects similar to Sanskrit, early Greek, and Latin. The noun inflected in the singular through seven cases: nominative, accusative, vocative, genitive, dative-locative, ablative, and instrumental, and some cases merged with others in the plural. The verb exhibited two primary tenses, present-future and past. Once scholars had mastered the basic grammar of the language, they made rapid progress in the reading of uncomplicated historical and legal texts.

Archaeological excavations have continued at Boghazköy—with interruptions for the two world wars—every year down to the present. The excavation directors have been Hugo Winckler, Kurt Bittel, and Peter Neve. More than ninety volumes of cuneiform tablets have been published. Texts of all types—historical narratives, state treaties, letters, a law code, myths and stories, prayers, descriptions of rituals and festivals, and descriptions of oracular techniques—have been edited and analyzed. Grammars and glossaries of Hittite and other closely related languages spoken in Anatolia in Hittite times have been written. Compendia of personal and divine names, as well as geographical names, have been compiled. The research of the past seventy years has put the discipline of Hittitology on a truly sound footing.

History

It is generally thought that the Hittites migrated into Anatolia from somewhere to the north and east. No one knows whether they came over the Caucasus or the Bosphorus. The time of their arrival is also uncertain, although to allow time for the linguistic differentiation between the sister languages Hittite, Luwian, and Palaic it has been suggested that all Indo-European groups were in Anatolia by around 2300.[1] The earliest Old Hittite kings, Labarna I and Hattusili I, reigned during the eighteenth century. What is called the Old Kingdom lasted to the early fifteenth century, when a new dynasty of kings and queens with Hurrian personal names established itself in Hattusa. Some scholars call the period c. 1500–1380 the Middle Kingdom. Others, seeing no discontinuity with the period which followed, prefer the terms Early New Kingdom or Early Empire.

The year 1380 marks a new beginning. In this year Suppiluliuma I began his reign. Suppiluliuma put an end to the Hurrian kingdom of Mittanni in the region of the Upper Euphrates and brought extensive areas in North Syria under Hittite control. He made the Hittites the only real geopolitical rivals of the Egyptian pharaohs. The Egypto-Hittite rivalry reached a climax in 1300, when the armies of the two empires fought to a standoff near the city

---

[1] The dates used in this survey all refer to millennia before the rise of Christianity, are approximate, and follow the standard histories written over the past twenty-five years. No account has been taken of the most recent attempts to establish an absolute chronology for Hittite history (Wilhelm 1987; Astour 1989)

of Kadesh on the Orontes River. It having become clear that neither side could dominate the other by military force, diplomatic cooperation increased, leading to a treaty between the pharaoh Ramses II and King Hattusili III c. 1270. This treaty was accompanied by a marriage between Hattusili's daughter and Ramses.

The Hittites' new enemy in the 1200s was Assyria, which had revived after the destruction of Mittanni. Wars between Hatti and Assyria occurred during the reign of Hattusili's successor, Tudhaliya IV. Hattusa fell c. 1170 during the reign of Suppiluliuma II to unknown invaders. The credit is usually given to "Sea Peoples," an imprecise term which refers to peoples displaced from their earlier home to the west, who arrived on the coasts of the eastern Mediterranean seeking a new homeland (Sandars 1980; Singer 1988). The Egyptian pharaoh Ramses III fought them in the Nile Delta lands. It is widely believed that the Philistines mentioned in the Hebrew Bible formed a part of that larger group. It is uncertain, however, that the Sea Peoples were the immediate cause of the fall of Hattusa. Weakened by wars with Assyria and a famine, the Hittites could have succumbed to their old nemesis, the nomadic Kaskaean hordes from northern Anatolia. What is certain is that the capital was captured, razed, and never rebuilt by the Hittites.

Civilization

"Civilization" is a slippery term. Usually it connotes a configuration of customs and beliefs which characterize a large social group. But should the boundaries of "civilizations" be drawn geographically? Was there a Western Anatolian, a Central Anatolian, and a North Syrian civilization during the Hittite period? Or should the boundaries be drawn ethnolinguistically: Hittite-Nesite civilization, Luwian civilization, Palaic civilization, Hurrian civilization? On analogy with later periods of Anatolian history, we may assume that throughout Asia Minor and North Syria certain common legal, religious, and cultic norms provided a sufficient basis for a "civilization."

Hittite international law preserved the diversity of local legal traditions. Hittite cultic practices can now be seen in texts composed in the Babylonian language as far from Hattusa as Meskene in Syria (Klengel 1988; Laroche 1988). The Hurrian myths of the Kumarbi Cycle are set in Upper Meso-potamia (Urkis, Kummiya), North Syria (Tuttul) and along the eastern coast of the Mediterranean (Mount Hazzi = Mount Kasios). Hittite rulers prided themselves on the internal diversity of their culture. Religious syncretism provided the means to assimilate new groups. Gods of the Hattians, Luwians, and Hurrians who performed similar functions or showed similar traits were equated for purposes of official worship. The Hittite state survived for six hundred years because of its adaptability. Although important changes occurred between the Old and New Kingdoms, it is the thread of continuity rather than the occasional trace of discontinuity which is significant.

The Myths

The texts assembled and translated here are mythological: that is, they deal—in some cases exclusively—with the divine figures who formed the focus of Hittite worship. I have organized them into four divisions. The first two divisions include texts from the Old Hittite and New Hittite periods in which mortals enjoy only a peripheral role in the narrative. In the third division I have assembled a few interesting examples of legendary narratives in which both gods and mortals play important roles. Indeed, in these stories the focus is on human actions, the gods intervening only occasionally. Although this literary category has sometimes been judged irrelevant to mythology proper (see, e.g., Güterbock 1961), I have followed Bernabé (1987) in including these texts in my third division. Such compositions are also narratives that relate in a straightforward manner the intervention of gods in human affairs, and they belong stylistically to the same type of literature. Recognition of this fact is implicit in the editing of Appu and Hedammu in the same volume by Siegelová (1971). In my fourth division I have presented the Hittite version of a Canaanite myth whose basic outline is familiar from the texts of the Baal cycle of myths found in the city of Ugarit.

On the Method of Translation

Although Hittite texts are no more difficult to translate than those of any other "dead" language, scholars have adopted various styles of translation. To accompany a formal edition of a Hittite text—including hand copies or photos of the texts, transliteration, and commentary—a scholar may employ a very literal translation, imitate the word order of the original composition, and render certain Hittite words in transcription. When writing for a circle of specialists, one can assume a great deal of common understanding of Hittite history and customs. If a word is partially broken on the tablet but is identifiable, a Hittitologist will enclose the restored portion of the word in square brackets. Hans Güterbock's translation of the Song of Ullikummi (1952) illustrates this style.

The guidelines established for the series Writings from the Ancient World specify that translators avoid the more technical approach. The translation is to be couched in smooth, idiomatic English. The meanings of rare words are to be guessed at. Partially preserved words are not interrupted by brackets. I have observed these guidelines. Where the meaning of the passage is clear to me, I have allowed myself more freedom to use a smooth, idiomatic

English. Where the context is poorly preserved or the meaning is uncertain, I have been more cautious, translating known words more literally. I have rarely resorted to conjecture. Writing for a general audience, I am unable to provide scholarly justification for innovative translations offered here. Some of these are supported in *The Hittite Dictionary of the Oriental Institute of the University of Chicago*. In broken passages, where vital parts of the sentence (subject, verb) are missing, it would obviously assist the reader to know what nouns are marked by their case endings as subject, direct object, indirect object. If the grammatical case can be conveyed by English word order, I have preferred this method to "tagging" the translation. But in some cases it has been necessary to write "[accusative]" or to resolve the ambiguity of English "you" by "you [plural]" or "you [singular]." Occasionally I have had to designate symbols or deified concepts as proper names. Text 2 §29 is an example. In such cases capitalization indicates that the words are a name.

On the Transliteration and Pronunciation of Words and Names

To simplify the typography of this book I have employed an ordinary "s" to render Hittite "š," and an ordinary "h" to render "ḫ." Since it is still not absolutely clear whether the "s" was pronounced as English "s" or "sh," and the "h" as English "h" or the throat-clearing sound "kh," I do not insist on any one pronunciation here. But the reader should be warned that in writing "sh" for the more usual Hittitological "šḫ" I am indicating not the single English sound "sh," but two distinct, successive sounds ("s" + "h" or "sh" + "kh"). The same is true for Hittite "th," in which the "t" and "h" represent two distinct, consecutive sounds ("Zithariya" is to be pronounced "Zit-ha-ri-ya," not "Zi-tha-ri-ya").

Proper names appearing entirely in capital letters represent what are called ideograms (or logograms). These are Sumerian (roman capitals such as LAMMA, ERESHKIGAL) or Akkadian (italicized capitals such as *ISHTAR*) names, which stand for unknown Hittite equivalents. To distinguish these names from native Hittite ones we write them in capital letters. Since in the Sumerian and Akkadian languages there is an important distinction between "s" and "sh," I have indicated the sound "sh" with the letters "SH": thus, *ISHTAR* and ERESHKIGAL. Certain untranslatable common nouns written with logograms are also employed in the translations (e.g., the GUDU-priest). In accordance with the series guidelines, I have not transcribed these logograms as required in technical editions. The divine name ^{d}ZA.BA$_4$.BA$_4$ is written ZABABA. The clerical title ^{LU2}GUDU$_{12}$ is written GUDU. The determinative for deity is omitted from all divine names: LAMMA, not ^{d}LAMMA.

In almost all cases the paragraph divisions within the translations reflect divisions made by Hittite scribes on the original tablets. I have numbered the paragraphs to facilitate cross referencing within the volume and referencing these translations in other publications. The line numbers in parentheses which follow the paragraph numbers refer to the Hittite texts. They serve the needs of persons who may wish to verify the translations.

Translations

I

Old Anatolian Myths

Introduction

The myths in this section, although none of their extant copies derives from the Old Hittite period, are thought to have been current during that early period. Although we do not yet possess any version of the stories in a language other than Hittite, most scholars assume that they were adopted by the Hittites at an early time from the indigenous population groups of Central Anatolia, principally the so-called Hattians. In contrast, the myths of our second division were translated into Hittite, and probably adapted in certain ways, from Hurrian versions. Unilingual Hurrian mythological texts have been found in Hattusa, but they are difficult to translate. To date, very little has been deduced from them which clarifies the Hittite versions. No tablet datable to the Old Kingdom has yet appeared which contains a Hittite mythological text of Hurrian origin, but the recent recovery in Hattusa of a Hurrian–Hittite bilingual version of a literary text with mythological sections which dates from the Middle Hittite period shows the probable *terminus a quo* for the Kumarbi Cycle of myths.

In his catalogue of Hittite texts, as well as in his transliteration of Hittite mythological texts, the eminent French Hittitologist Emmanuel Laroche distinguished Anatolian myths from foreign (i.e., extra-Anatolian) myths. Güterbock (1961) has observed how the myths of the first group (here Texts 1–13) tend to be rather simple, unsophisticated stories. Stylistically they lack the polished structure and the abundant formulae and similes of the myths in group two. The vanishing god myths do indeed contain abundant similes in the portions containing analogic spells (Text 2, version 1, §§10–15), but these reinforce the magic, and do not serve the interests of artistry. Although the myths of the Kumarbi Cycle (Texts 14–18) are called "songs" in the native terminology, which suggests at least some artistic pretension, the Old Anatolian myths have no such characterization.

The Anatolian myths tend to serve the interests of the cult. The Illuyanka stories (Text 1) formed the cult legend of the Purulli Festival. The stories of Telipinu (Texts 2–5, 7–9, and 13) and other vanishing deities were associated with rituals to entice the offended deity to return in solicitude to his land and people. This is not so with the myths of Hurrian origin. They may not be pure and simple *belles lettres*, but they probably had a looser connection with ritual and worship than the myths of Hattian origin. Judging from the advance notices (Neu 1988a, 1988c, Otten 1984a, 1984b,

9

1986) of the content of the Hurro-Hittite bilingual not yet published by Neu, its mythological narrative served in part to support the observance of certain religio-social obligations connected with what in other ancient Near Eastern cultures was termed the periodic remission of debts and release of debt slaves (Babylonian *andurāru,* Hebrew *derôr,* Greek *seisachtheia*). But this is quite a different picture from the ritual-supported narratives of the Anatolian myths.

As might be expected, the geographical background of the Anatolian stories is local. This is especially evident in Illuyanka, where place-names like Kiskilussa, Ziggaratta, Nerik, Kastama, and Tanipiya tie the action to familiar terrain to the north of Hattusa. Hittite geographical names are less common in the vanishing god stories, but even there one finds mention of Lihzina and Hattusa. In contrast, the myths of Hurrian origin mention cities and lands of North Syria (Mount Hazzi, Tuttul) and Mesopotamia (Urkis, Kummiya).

Although the myths of foreign origin are more polished literary creations, this is not to say that the Anatolian myths have no subtlety (Hoffner 1975). Both versions of the Illuyanka stories show consequences flowing from the major plot of the Storm God's recovery of his strength and defeat of the serpent. These consequences fall tragically upon a mortal who is the instrument of the Storm God's victory. In both stories this mortal is confronted with a conflict of allegiances, a kind of moral dilemma. In the first version, the ultimate consequence of his decision is unknown because of textual breaks, but in version 2 the decision of the human son of the Storm God costs him his life. At least in the second instance, where the consequence is clear, it is not too much to claim that the author intended the audience to feel the tragedy. Such a plot may not be "literary" in the strict sense, but it is surely evidence for good storytelling technique! Moreover, since this subordinate plot line, unlike the main plot of the Storm God's recovery, has no obvious relationship to the cult applications, it would seem to indicate that the stories were also told to entertain, not just for the benefit of theology.

Of course, the last sentence is only valid if the main cult application of the Illuyanka tales was to the disablement and recovery of the Storm God himself. This has usually been assumed to be the case. Since the myths of the vanishing deity type (Texts 2–8 and 13) concern a certain deity who is incapacitated, kidnapped, or infuriated so as to depart in a huff, all of which makes it impossible for that deity to perform his function for the benefit of mortals and gods, the Illuyanka tales fit the pattern better if we regard the conflict between Storm God and serpent as their principal focus. Nevertheless, the recent attempt by Pecchioli Daddi (1987) to attribute to the Purulli Festival certain cult texts about the deity Teteshapi, whom she identifies with the goddess Inara, would perhaps suggest that the role played in Text 1 by that goddess was not considered subordinate by the Hittites themselves.

====================== **1. The Illuyanka Tales** ======================

These simple tales, taken over from the Hattian people, attribute a poor spring to the defeat and incapacitation of their chief deity, the Storm God, by an evil and powerful reptile. Reptiles are not universally symbols of evil and destruction: In

Egypt the uraeus serpent protected the pharaoh from evil. But clearly in Hittite culture, as in Babylonia and ancient Israel, serpents usually represented evil. In both versions of the myth, the Storm God needs the help of a mortal and a trick in order to regain supremacy over the serpent. These stories were probably told or sung during the course of the Purulli Festival, about which we know relatively little outside of these stories. If Pecchioli Daddi (1987) is right in including the Teteshapi cult texts under the rubric of Purulli, we know more. Since Pecchioli Daddi has announced further publications on this subject (*Newsletter for Anatolian Studies* 4 [1988] 17), we will soon see what results from mining this new source. Haas (1988a) has sought to build upon Pecchioli Daddi's ideas.

Although the Illuyanka text shows much linguistic archaism, which suggests that the narratives go back at least to the Old Hittite period (c. 1750–1500), the surviving copies date only from the New Kingdom (c. 1500–1190).

Version 1

In the first story the serpent is a land creature who emerges from a hole in the ground. The defeated and disabled Storm God calls for a feast, at which his daughter, the goddess Inara, a goddess of the wild animals of the steppe land, in partnership with a mortal man, Hupasiya, tricks the serpent and renders him powerless. Haas (1982: 45, 111) has characterized Hupasiya as a *Jahreskönig*, a king who with his priestess queen guarantees the flourishing of livestock and vegetation. In suggesting that there are allusions in Hupasiya to ritual regicide, Haas seems to assume that Hupasiya is eventually killed. But these interpretations rest upon a superficial use of comparative evidence and lack a proper foundation in solid textual evidence from the Hittite sources. Nothing in the narrative suggests that Hupasiya becomes a king, and it is still uncertain that he is killed. It also goes beyond the present evidence to assert that Hupasiya's sleeping with Inara was a *hieros gamos* (sacred marriage) (Haas 1982), the nature (and even existence!) of which in other ancient Near Eastern cultures is still seriously questioned. In the first version of the story all the characters have names, and the earthly action is set in or near known Anatolian cities, such as Tarukka and Ziggaratta.

§1 (A i 1–4) (This is) the text of the Purulli (Festival) for the [. . .] of the Storm God of heaven, according to Kella, [the GUDU-priest] of the Storm God of Nerik: When they speak thus—

§2 (A i 5–8) "Let the land prosper (and) thrive, and let the land be protected" — and when it prospers and thrives, they perform the Purulli Festival.

§3 (A i 9–11) When the Storm God and the serpent fought each other in Kiskilussa, the serpent defeated the Storm God.

§4 (A i 12–14) Then the Storm God invoked all the gods: "Come together to me." So Inara prepared a feast.

§5 (A i 15–18) She prepared everything on a grand scale: storage vessels full of wine, storage vessels of *marnuwan* beer and *walhi* drink. In the vessels she prepared abundant (refreshment).

§6 (A i 19–20) Then [Inara] went [to] (the town of) Ziggaratta and found a mortal named Hupasiya.

§7 (A i 21–23) Inara spoke as follows to Hupasiya: "I am about to do such-and-such a thing. You join with me."

§8 (A i 24–26) Hupasiya replied as follows to Inara: "If I may sleep with you, then I will come and perform your heart's (desire)." [So] he slept with her.

§9 (B i 3–8) Then Inara led Hupasiya off and concealed him. Inara dressed herself up and called the serpent up from its hole, (saying:) "I'm preparing a feast. Come eat and drink."

§10 (B i 9–12) The serpent and [his offspring] came up, and they ate and drank. They drank up every vessel, so that they became drunk.

§11 (B i 13–16) Now they do not want to go back down into their hole again. Hupasiya came and tied up the serpent with a rope.

§12 (B i 17–18) The Storm God came and killed the serpent, and the gods were with him.

§13 (C i 14–22) Then Inara built a house on a rock (outcropping) in (the town of) Tarukka (north of Hattusa) and settled Hupasiya in the house. Inara repeatedly instructed him: "When I go out to the open country, don't look out the window. If you look out, you will see your wife and children."

§14 (C i 23–24) When twenty days had passed, he looked out the window and saw his wife and children.

§15 (C i 25–27) When Inara returned from the open country, he began to weep, (saying): "Let me go back home."

§16 (A ii 9–14) Inara said [to Hupasiya: . . .] away [. . .] by means of an offense [. . .] the Storm God, the meadow [. . .] she [. . .] and him [. . .]. [*Text broken.*[1]]

§17 (A ii 15–20) Inara [went] to (the town of) Kiskilussa. How did the hand of the king establish her house and the [. . .] of the watery abyss? Because we celebrate the first Purulli [Festival], the [hand] of the king [. . . s] the [river(?)] of the watery abyss of Inara.

§18 (A ii 21–24) The (divine) mountain Zaliyanu is first (in rank) of all (the gods). When he has granted rain in Nerik, the Staff Bearer brings thick bread from Nerik.

§19 (A ii 25–29) He asked Zaliyanu for rain,[2] so he brings it to him (namely) the [thick] bread. . . .

[*Several damaged lines followed by a gap of about forty lines. A double line marks the end of the first composition on the tablet.*]

Version 2

In the second story the characters have no names but are identified by functional expressions, such as "daughter of a poor man" and "son of the Storm God." No geographical names occur. The two battles of the Storm God and the serpent take place at an unspecified sea. The Storm God's ruse involves a special type of marriage known from the Hittite laws.[3] If a young suitor was too poor to pay a bride-price for a wife, he could offer himself as a "live-in" husband to a wealthy father-in-law in exchange for a "bride-price" paid to himself. The Storm God's son thus finds himself in a classic situation of divided loyalty: he is son of the Storm God but also live-in son-in-law of the serpent. His agonizing choice costs him his life. The fact that the Storm God's mortal son was also the son of "the daughter of a poor man" helps us to understand why such a marriage arrangement would be necessary for him. Pecchioli Daddi has pointed out that "the daughter of a poor man" plays a role in certain cult texts of the deity Teteshapi, whom she identifies with Inara (Pecchioli Daddi 1987).

§21 (D iii 2–5) That which [Kella, the GUDU-priest] said: [First] the serpent defeated [the Storm God] and took [his heart and eyes], and the Storm God [feared(?)] him.

§22 (A iii 4–8) So he took as his wife the daughter of a poor man and sired a son. When (the son) grew up, he took the daughter of the serpent as his wife.

§23 (A iii 9–12) The Storm God repeatedly instructed him: "When you go (to live in) the house of your wife, demand from them (my) heart and eyes (as a bride-price)."

§24 (A iii 13–19) So when he went, he demanded from them the heart, and they gave it to him. After that he demanded from them the eyes, and they gave those too to him. He brought them to his father, the Storm God, and the Storm God took back (his) heart and his eyes.

§25 (A iii 20–28) When he was again sound in body as before, he went again to the sea to do battle. When he gave him battle, and he at last began to defeat the serpent, the Storm God's son was with the serpent and called up to his father in the sky:

§26 (A iii 29–33) "Include me with them; have no pity on me." So the Storm God killed (both) the serpent and his own son. And that Storm God [. . .].

§27 (A iii 34–35) Thus says Kella, [the GUDU-priest of the Storm God of Nerik]: When the gods [. . .].

[*Gap of undetermined length.*]

§28 (D iv 1–4) For the GUDU-priest they made the first gods last, and the last ones first.

§29 (D iv 5–7) The cult provision for Zalinuwa is much. Zalinuwa is his (i.e., Zashapuna's) wife. Zashapuna is greater than the Storm God of Nerik.

§30 (D iv 8–10) Thus speak those same gods to the GUDU-priest Tahpurili: "When we go to Nerik, where shall we take seats?"

§31 (D iv 11–16) The GUDU-priest Tahpurili speaks as follows: "When you sit on basalt throne(s), and the GUDU-priest(s) cast lots, whichever GUDU-priest holds (the image of) Zaliyanu will be seated on a basalt throne which is set above the spring/basin.

§32 (D iv 14–17) All the gods will assemble and cast lots. And of all the gods of the town of Kastama, Zashapuna will be the greatest."

§33 (D iv 18–21) Because she is the wife of Zaliyanu, and Tazzuwasi is (his) concubine, these three men (i.e., unnamed GUDU-priests?) remain in the town of Tanipiya.

§34 (A iv 22–23) Thereafter in the town of Tanipiya a field is given by the king.

§35 (A iv 24–28) Six *kapunu*-measures of field, one *kapunu* of vineyard, a house and threshing floor, three buildings for the servants. So it is on the tablet. I am reverent with regard to the words. I have spoken this (truly).

§36 (colophon of A) Tablet one, complete, of the word of Kella, the GUDU-priest. Pihaziti, [the scribe], wrote it under the supervision of Walwaziti, the chief scribe.

=========== 2. The Disappearance of Telipinu ===========

Version 1

With this story we begin the section of Old Hittite myths dealing with deities who become alienated from the land and people whom they normally protect, leave their posts, and go into hiding. The effects of their departure upon gods, humans, animals, and plants are graphically portrayed. The Telipinu myth is the best preserved and most familiar of this type. Telipinu was the son of the great Storm God. His competence lay in fostering agriculture, particularly cereal culture. Compare Text 7, §6. He shows his anger with thunder and lightning (Text 2, version 1, §16). Therefore, although his usual designation is by his Hattic name, Telipinu, he is clearly a Storm God. Hence, the myth which relates his anger and disappearance shares much with those which concern the disappearance of other storm gods (Texts 3, 4, and 5). When, however, it is the Sun God who disappears (Text 7), the effects on nature are predictable. Without the sun's warming rays, the land falls under the power of the personified Jack Frost (Hittite *hahhimas*), who paralyzes everything and "dries up" the waters. In many of the stories the gods organize a mass search by their own membership; this, however, fails. A swiftly flying, sharp-eyed eagle is then dispatched on aerial reconnaissance, but it too finds nothing. The wise Mother Goddess Hannahanna then sends out the tiny bee, whom the gods think unlikely to succeed. The bee finds the hiding deity, stings him awake, pacifies him by spreading soothing wax on the welt, and brings him back home.

§1 (A i 1–4) Telipinu [. . . screamed]: "Let there be no intimidating language." [Then] he drew [on the right shoe] on his left foot, and the left [shoe on his right foot].

§2 (A i 5–9) Mist seized the windows. Smoke [seized] the house. In the fireplace the logs were stifled. [At the altars] the gods were stifled. In the sheep pen the sheep were stifled. In the cattle barn the cattle were stifled. The mother sheep rejected her lamb. The cow rejected her calf.

§3 (A i 10–15) Telipinu too went away and removed grain, animal fecundity, luxuriance, growth, and abundance to the steppe, to the meadow. Telipinu too went into the moor and blended with the moor. Over him the *halenzu*-plant grew. Therefore barley (and) wheat no longer ripen. Cattle, sheep, and humans no longer become pregnant. And those (already) pregnant cannot give birth.

§4 (A i 16–20) The mountains and the trees dried up, so that the shoots do not come (forth). The pastures and the springs dried up, so that famine broke out in the land. Humans and gods are dying of hunger. The Great Sun God made a feast and invited the Thousand Gods. They ate but couldn't get enough. They drank but couldn't quench their thirst.

§5 (A i 21–25) The Storm God thought about (i.e., remembered) his son Telipinu: "My son Telipinu is not there. He became enraged and removed everything good." The great and small gods began to search for Telipinu. The Sun God sent the swift eagle: "Go search the high mountains."

§6 (A i 26–31) "Search the deep valleys. Search the Blue Deep." The eagle went, but didn't find him. But he brought back a message to the Sun God: "I couldn't find Telipinu, the noble god." The Storm God said to Hannahanna: "How shall we act? We are going to die of hunger." Hannahanna said to the Storm God: "Do something, Storm God. Go search for Telipinu yourself."

§7 (A i 32–35) The Storm God began to search for Telipinu. In his city (the Storm God) [grasps] the city gate, but can't manage to open it. Instead the Storm God broke his hammer and his wedge(?). He wrapped himself up (in his garment) and sat down. Hannahanna sent [a bee]: "Go search for Telipinu."

§8 (A i 36–39) [The Storm God] said [to Hannahanna]: "Since the great and small gods have been searching for him, but haven't found him, will this [bee find] him? His wings are small, and he himself is small, and in addition he is. . . ."

§9 (A ii 3–8) Telipinu [. . .]. The malt and "beer bread" is. . . . He . . . ed. He cut off goodness(?) [. . .] at the gate. May the sweet odor [invoke you], Telipinu. Frustrated, [may you be] relaxed.

§10 (A ii 9–11) Here [lies] water of. . . . [May it . . .] your soul, O Telipinu. So [turn] in favor toward the king.

§11 (A ii 12–14) Here lies *galaktar*. May [your soul, O Telipinu], be made tranquil. Here [lies] *parhuenas*-fruit. May (its) essence(?) implore him, [namely, Telipinu].

§12 (A ii 15–18) Here lie *samama*-nuts. Let [. . .] be manifest(?). Here [lie] figs. Just as [a fig] is sweet, so let [your soul], Telipinu, become sweet in the same way.

§13 (A ii 19–21) Just as an olive [holds] its oil in its heart, [just as a grape] holds its wine in its heart, so you, Telipinu, must hold goodness in your soul and heart in the same way.

§14 (A ii 22–27) Here lies resinous wood(?). Let it anoint [your soul], Telipinu. Just as malt and beer bread are united in "soul," let your soul, [Telipinu], be united in the same way with the words of (these) mortals. [Just as wheat] is pure, so let Telipinu, (namely) his soul, become pure in the same way. [Just as] honey is sweet, as ghee is mild, so let the soul of Telipinu become sweet in the same way, and let it become mild in the same way.

§15 (A ii 28–32) I have just sprinkled your paths, Telipinu, with sweet oil. Set out, Telipinu, on paths sprinkled with sweet oil. Let *sahis* (boughs) and *happuriyasas* (boughs) be pleasant. Just as reed(?) (and) . . . are pleasant, so you be pleasant, Telipinu, in the same way.

§16 (A ii 33–36, iii 1–2) Telipinu came in anger. He thunders together with lightning. Below he strikes the Dark Earth. Kamrusepa saw him and moved (for) herself [with(?)] the eagle's wing. She stopped it, namely, anger. She stopped it, the wrath. She stopped [sin]. She stopped sullenness.

§17 (A iii 3–7) Kamrusepa says to the gods: "Go, O gods. Now tend the Sun God's sheep for Hapantali, and cut out twelve rams, so that I may treat Telipinu's *karas*-grains. I have taken for myself a basket (with) a thousand small holes. And upon it I have poured *karas*-grains, the "rams of Kamrusepa."

§18 (A iii 8–12) And I have made a burning back and forth over Telipinu, on one side and on the other. And I have taken from Telipinu, from his body, his evil; I have taken his sin; I have taken his anger; I have taken his wrath; I have taken his pique(?); I have taken his sullenness.

§19 (A iii 13–20) Telipinu is angry. His soul and essence were stifled (like burning) brushwood. Just as they burned these sticks of brushwood, may the anger, wrath, sin, and sullenness of Telipinu likewise burn up. [And] just as [malt] is ineffective, so that they don't carry it to the field and use it as seed, (as) they don't make it into bread and deposit it in the Seal House, so may the anger, wrath, sin, and sullenness of Telipinu likewise become ineffective.

§20 (A iii 21–23) Telipinu is angry. His soul and . . . are a burning fire. And just as this fire [is extinguished], so [may] (his) anger, wrath, and sullenness likewise [be extinguished].

§21 (A iii 24–27) Telipinu, let anger go. [Let] wrath [go]. Let sullenness go. And just as (the water in) a drain pipe doesn't flow backward, so may [the anger, wrath], and sullenness of Telipinu likewise not come back.

§22 (A iii 28–34) The gods [are sitting(?) in the place] of convocation under the hawthorn tree. And under the hawthorn tree long [. . . s are . . .] And all the gods are sitting: [Papaya], Istustaya, the Fate Goddesses, the Mother Goddesses, the Dark Goddess, Miyatanzipa, Telipinu, the Tutelary Deity, Hapantali [and . . .]. I have treated the gods under (the hawthorn) for long years [. . .]. I have purified him.

§23 (C 9-12) [I have taken] evil from Telipinu's body. I have taken his [anger. I have taken his] wrath. I have taken his [sin]. [I have taken] sullenness. I have taken [the evil] tongue. [I have taken] the evil [fetter].

[*The remainder of column iii is broken away. In what follows the thorny hawthorn tree is addressed.*]

§24 (A iv 1-3) [The ox passes under you], and you pull its lock of hair. The sheep passes under you, and you pull its tuft of wool. Pull the anger, wrath, sin, and sullenness from Telipinu too.

§25 (A iv 4-7) The Storm God comes, full of anger, and the Man of the Storm God stops him. The bowl comes, and the wooden . . . stops it. In addition may my mortal words likewise stop Telipinu's anger, wrath, and sullenness.

§26 (A iv 8-13) May Telipinu's anger, wrath, sin, and sullenness depart. May the house release it. May the middle . . . release it. May the window release it. May the hinge ‹release it.› May the middle courtyard release it. May the city gate release it. May the gate complex release it. May the King's Road release it. May it not go into the fruitful field, garden, or forest. May it go the route of the Sun Goddess (of the Dark Earth).

§27 (A iv 14-19) The gatekeeper opened the seven doors. He drew back the seven bars. Down in the Dark Earth stand bronze *palhi*-vessels. Their lids are of lead. Their latches are of iron. That which goes into them doesn't come up again; it perishes therein. So may they seize Telipinu's anger, wrath, sin, and sullenness, and may they not come back (here).

§28 (A iv 20-26) Telipinu came back home to his house and took account of his land. The mist released the windows. The smoke released the house. The altars were in harmony again with the gods. The fireplace released the log. In the sheepfold he released the sheep. In the cattle barn he released the cattle. Then the mother looked after her child. The sheep looked after her lamb. The cow looked after her calf. And Telipinu too ‹looked after› the king and queen and took account of them in respect to life, vigor, and longevity.

§29 (A iv 27-31) Telipinu took account of the king. Before Telipinu there stands an *eyan*-tree (or pole). From the *eyan* is suspended a hunting bag (made from the skin) of a sheep. In (the bag) lies Sheep Fat.[4] In it lie (symbols) of Animal Fecundity and of Wine. In it lie (symbols of) Cattle and Sheep. In it lie Longevity and Progeny.

§30 (A iv 32-35) In it lies The Gentle Message of the Lamb. In it lie . . . and. . . . In it lies. . . . In it lies The Right Shank. In it lie Plenty, Abundance, and Satiety.

[*The remainder of column iv is broken away. This is the end of version 1 of the Telipinu myth.*]

Version 2

The beginning of column i is broken away. Most of the restorations in the following sections are drawn from version 1. §§1–2 are paralleled by version 1 §§3–4.

§1 (A i 2–3) [Cattle, sheep], and humans [no longer become pregnant]. [And even those who] do [cannot give birth].

§2 (A i 4–6) In the [land] famine broke out. [The Great Sun God made a feast and invited] the great gods [and the lesser] gods. [They ate but] couldn't get enough. They drank but [couldn't quench their thirst].

§3 (A i 7–11) [The Storm God] said to the gods: "[My son is missing]. He became enraged and [removed everything good], so that famine broke out in the land." The great gods and the lesser gods began [to search for] Telipinu, but [they did] not [find] him.

§4 (A i 12–16) The Sun God sent the swift eagle: "[Go] search for Telipinu." The eagle went. It searched [the springs(?). It searched] the rivers. But it didn't find him. So it brought back a report to the Sun God: "I didn't find him."[5]

§5 (B ii 4–9) Hannahanna sent a bee: "You go search for [my son] Telipinu. When you find [him], sting his hands and feet and make him stand up. Then take wax and wipe him off. Then purify him and make him holy again. Then conduct him back here to me."

§6 (B ii 10–14) The Storm God said to Hannahanna: "Now the great gods and the lesser gods were searching for him, but didn't find him. So will this bee go find him? Its wings are small. It too is small. And furthermore it is all by itself(?)."

§7 (B ii 15–19) [Hannahanna] said to the Storm God: "Desist. It will go find him." The bee [went]. It began to [search for Telipinu]. It searched the . . . [. . .]. It searched the [. . .] rivers. It searched the [. . .] springs. [. . .] [*The rest of this section is broken away.*]

§8 (D ii 1–12) [*In these two small, badly damaged paragraphs there is mention of "finding" Telipinu and "making him stand up," as well as a question "How shall we act?" and a statement "Telipinu became angry."*]

§9 (D ii 13–17) [. . .] says: "[Summon] the mortal. [Let him . . .] the . . . [on] Mount Ammuna. Let him move him. [Let] the eagle [approach and] move [him] with a wing. Let the mortal make [him] arise." The eagle [moved(?)] him with its wing.

§10 (D ii 18–20) They stopped him [. . .] sat down [. . .] and he previously [. . .].

§11 (D ii 21–26) Telipinu [. . .] sent: Go [. . .] head [. . .] with thick bread and libation [. . .] purify(?) [. . .].

§12 (C ii 1–3) [Here] lies [*galaktar* for you, Telipinu]. Let [the . . . s] be [pacified]. [Turn] in favor [toward the king, queen, and princes].

§13 (C ii 4–6) [Here] lies [*parhuenas*-fruit for you]. You [be . . . , and] be [invoked] for the king, queen, [and princes].

§14 (C ii 7–10) [Here] lies [The Right Shank for you. . . . And] as [. . . , and . . .], so in the same way [let it stand] . . . to you.

[*Several paragraphs too broken to read.*]

§15 (B iii 2–4) [Here] lies wax for you. Drive [Telipinu's] anger, wrath, [sin, and sullenness] out from your presence.

§16 (C iii 5–7) Here lies wheat for you. Just as (this) wheat is pure, let Telipinu's [heart and soul] become pure again in the same way.

§17 (C iii 8–17) Here lie malt and "beer bread" for you. Just as malt and "beer bread" blend in essence, so that their soul and heart become one, [so may . . .]. They get an angry person drunk with beer of [. . .], and his anger vanishes from him. They get a timid man drunk, and his timidity vanishes from him. Let [the malt and "beer bread"] get you drunk, [Telipinu, in the same way . . .] wrath [. . .] let it vanish [. . .].

§18 (A iv 1–2) [As the fire is extinguished], so [may] Telipinu's evil [anger, wrath, sin, and sullenness be extinguished] in the same way.

§19 (A iv 3–7) [O Telipinu], let go of anger, [let go of] wrath, let go of [sin] and sullenness. [As] (the water in) drain pipes doesn't flow backward, so may [the evil anger], wrath, sin, and [sullenness] of Telipinu likewise not come back.

§20 (D iii 3–14) May the evil anger, wrath, [sin], and sullenness go away. But may it not go into the fruitful field, the forest, or the garden. May it go on the road to the Dark Earth. Down in the Dark Earth stand iron *palhi*-vessels. Their lids are of lead. Whatever goes into them doesn't come up again; it perishes therein. So may Telipinu's evil anger, wrath, sullenness, and sin go into them and not come up again, but perish therein.

§21 (D iii 15–22) (Telipinu,) eat fine things; drink fine things. May (your) path, O Telipinu, be sprinkled with fine oil. Then set out upon it. May your bedding be (fragrant) *sahis* and *happuriyasas* (boughs). Then sleep upon it. As fragrant reed is pleasant, may you be pleasant also to the king and queen and to the land of Hatti. [*End of version 2.*]

Version 3

[*Only parts of columns ii and iii of a four-column tablet are preserved.*]

§1 (A ii 2–6) [". . . You, O bee, should look for Telipinu]. And when you find (him), sting [him on his hands and feet. Make] him stand up. [Take wax] and [wipe off] his eyes and his hands. Purify him and bring him back to me."

§2 (B ii 1–5) The bee searched the high mountains; it searched [the deep valleys; it searched the Blue] Deep. The honey was exhausted in its interior, [the . . .] was exhausted [in its . . .]. But [it found] him in a meadow in the town of Lihzina, in a forest. It stung [him] on his hands and feet, so that he got up.

§3 (B ii 6–12) [This is what] Telipinu said: "I was both angry and [sleeping]. [Why did] you [*plural*] [arouse] me when I was sleeping? Why did you make [me] talk, when I was sulking?" [Telipinu] became (even more) angry. [He . . . ed] the spring. . . . He drew the rivers and brooks(?). He [. . .]ed [the . . .] and made them leap/flee. [He . . . ed] the riverbanks. He knocked down [cities(?)]. He knocked down houses.

§4 (B ii 13–16) He destroyed people. He destroyed cattle and sheep. The gods . . . ed [. . .]. "Telipinu has become angry. [. . .] How shall we act? [How] shall we act?"

§5 (B ii 17–22) "Summon [*plural*] a human being and let him [. . .] . . . . Let the eagle [. . .]. Let him bring [him]." The eagle brought [him]. It [. . . ed] with its wing. They . . . ed [him and . . .]. [*The rest of column ii is lost in a break. The ends of lines of part of column iii remain. This section seems to describe the final success of the ritual to pacify the angry deity and restore prosperity to the cosmos.*]

§6 (A iii 4–8) [. . .] on his body parts [. . .] he expelled. [He dispelled(?)] anger, [wrath, sin, and sullenness], the evil fetter, [. . .], the envious eyes, [. . .]. He left [. . .] and [. . .]ed forth.

§7 (A iii 9–11) [. . .] brought forth [. . .] from the [. . . . He brought forth] grain, animal fecundity, [. . .], beneficial rains, beneficial winds. He brought forth all [. . .].

§8 (A iii 12–14) May [the . . .] wear out [the . . .]. May the apple tree [. . . the . . .] of the god [. . .]. May the *marsiggas*-tree [. . . the . . .] of [. . .]. His soul [. . .]. [*The rest of the tablet is broken away.*]

=========== **3. The Disappearance of the Storm God** ===========

§1 (A i 3–4) [Mist seized the windows. Smoke] seized [the house. In the hearth the logs] were stifled.

§2 (A i 5–7) [At the altars the gods were stifled]. In the sheepfold [the sheep were stifled. In the cattle barn the] cattle [were stifled. The ewe rejected her lamb. The cow] rejected her calf.

§3 (A i 8–13) [The Storm God of the Sky set out toward the steppe], the meadow, [and the moor(?). He carried off plenty, prosperity, and abundance. The Storm God departed], and barley [and wheat] no longer [ripened. Cattle, sheep], and humans did not [become pregnant]. And those who [were pregnant did not give birth] from that time.

§4 (A i 14–15) [The mountains] dried up. [The trees] dried up. And the shoots(?) [did not come forth. The pastures] dried up. The springs dried up.

§5 (A i 16–21) [The Sun God made] a feast and invited the Thousand Gods. [They ate], but couldn't get enough. They drank, but couldn't quench their thirst. [The Storm God's father] said: "My son [is not there]. He became angry and [carried off] everything good. He carried off grain, animal fecundity, abundance, plenty, and satiation."

§6 (A i 22–25) [All the gods] began to search for the Storm God. [. . .] sent the swift eagle: "Go search the high mountains. [Search] the deep valleys. Search the Blue Deep."

§7 (A i 26–29) [The eagle went], but did not find him. The swift eagle brought a report [to the Sun God]: "I searched the high mountains. I searched the deep valleys. [I searched] the Blue Deep, but I did not find him, the Storm God of the Sky."

§8 (A i 30–33) [The Storm God's] father went to his (i.e., the Storm God's) grandfather and said to him: "Who sinned [grievously(?)], so that the seed perished and everything dried up?" The grandfather said: "No one sinned; you alone sinned grievously(?)."

§9 (A i 34–36) The Storm God's father said: "It wasn't I who sinned." The grandfather said: "I will trace this matter out, and I will kill you. So go search for the Storm God."

§10 (A i 37–42) The Storm God's father went to Gulsa and Hannahanna. Thus said Gulsa and Hannahanna: "Why have you come, Storm God's father?" The Storm God's father replied: "The Storm God became angry, and everything dried up, and . . . perished. My father says: 'It is your fault. So I will trace the matter out and kill you.' Now how shall I act? What has happened?"

§11 (A i 43–46) Hannahanna said: "Don't be afraid. If it is your fault, I will make it right. And even if it is not your fault, I will still make it right. Go search for the Storm God [before] his grandfather hears."

§12 (A i 47–50) The Storm God's father said: "Then where shall I go search?" Hannahanna replied: "I will give him to you. Go bring [the bee] here, and I myself will instruct it. It will search for [the Storm God]."

§13 (B ii 16–20) The Storm God's father said: "But if the [great] gods and the [lesser gods] searched for him and didn't find him, will this [bee] find him? [Its wings] are tiny, and it itself is tiny, and furthermore it is all by itself(?).

[*Hannahanna replies, but the content is broken away.*]

§14 (A ii 2–6) The Storm God said: "Go [*plural*] [. . .]. Let His Majesty not bring me [water] of turning(?). Let him bring [. . .]. He who [. . . the . . .] of purification, took for himself an empty [. . .].

§15 (A ii 7–11) He poured His Majesty's water of turning(?) [. . .], and he [. . .]. And he went back to his father. [He brought grain, . . .], abundance, plenty, [and satiety]. And he proceeded [to . . .] in the courtyard.

§16 (A ii 12–16) What gods were in the house of his father [ate] and were satisfied. They [drank and quenched their thirst]. (The Storm God's father said:) "My son has come back home [and has brought back] grain, . . . , [abundance, plenty], and satiety."

[*Text breaks off for the rest of column ii.*]

§17 (A iii 1–2) [I have taken a basket (with) a thousand small holes. I have poured out the *karas*-grains, the "rams] of Kamrusepa."

§18 (A iii 3–6) [Out] over the Storm God [I have made a burning this way and that. I have taken his evil from the body] of the Storm God. I have taken his sin. [I have taken his anger and wrath.] I have taken his pique(?). [I have taken sullenness.]

§19 (A iii 7–12) The Storm God's wrath, [his soul and body] were stifled [like kindling wood. Just as they burn] these [pieces of kindling wood], may the Storm God's anger and wrath, [sin and sullenness] burn up in the same way. The Storm God's wrath, his soul and body, are a blazing fire. And just as this fire [is extinguished, so may] his anger, wrath, and sullenness [be extinguished in the same way].

═══ 4. Sacrifice and Prayer to the Storm God of Nerik ═══

§1 (obv. 1–4) If the Storm God of Nerik has [gone] from the city, they summon him from the cities of Nera (and) Lalla as follows. [. . .] the GUDU-priest goes to Nera and Lalla and sacrifices one sheep to the Storm God of Nerik and [. . . sheep] to the ERESHKIGAL goddess, to (the god) Uruzimu, and to the eternal deities. They slaughter the sheep down in a pit.

§2 (obv. 5–11) Three thick loaves of five units (each), twenty thick loaves of twenty units (each), twenty thick loaves of thirty units (each), three *SUTU*-measures of pure porridge—each thick loaf is made like a lunar crescent. The beer supplier of the city Takuppasa gives three jugs of *walhi*-beer and three jugs of *marnuwan* beer. The wine suppliers give three jugs of wine. They break the thick loaves. They fill the rhytons. And concurrently he speaks the word three times. He scatters (fragments of) thick loaves, beer, wine (and) liver in small quantities down into the pit. The GUDU-priest calls (in the Hattic language) three times down into the pit: *wi wi purusael purusael.* Concurrently he again speaks the word:

§3 (obv. 12–17) "The Storm God of Nerik became angry and went down into the pit. He [went] into the dark [four corners] and [. . .] to(?) the bloody, bloodstained, . . . [. . .] mortals. In Nerik the son of Sulikatti [turned(?)] his eyes to the Storm God of the Sky. He . . . ed rocks. The Storm God of Nerik [. . . ed] them, namely, birth, life, and longevity, from [the Tabarna-king (and) the Tawannanna-queen]."

§4 (obv. 18–23) "Let them summon [him . . .]. Let him turn himself [. . .] to the Dark Earth. Let him come [. . .]. Let him open the gates of the Dark Earth [. . .]. Before him/it [let . . .]. Let them [bring(?)] the Storm God of

Nerik up from the Dark Earth [. . .]. Hand over the War God of the city of [. . .]. Let him come and before [the . . .] bring itemized lists(?)."

§5 (obv. 24–32) "Lo, he is calling you, [O Storm God] to be Invoked. Let the *surasuras*-bird come. Hear it. [Say(?)] to Wuruntemu: 'Hear it.' Take it to heart. O noble (one), rise from the Marassanta River. May they say to him: 'O son of Sulinkatte, come up from the dark four corners, from the deep wave. Turn back to Nerik. Look upon the Tabarna-king, the Tawananna-queen [with kindly eyes]. On this day come to Nerik. . . . May the Storm God of Nerik enter. May [Wuruntemu] take [out] irritation from before [his mind]. May you release there [. . .].'"

§6 (obv. 33–36) ["To(?)] your mother [may you give . . .], vigor, long years, prosperity of the lands [. . .]. The goods of(?) the *dahangas*-room (are) in place. [May you come] up, O [Storm God of Nerik]. May you let the city of Nerik into (your) [soul]."

§7 (obv. 37–39, rev. 1–6) "To your mother [. . .] your [mother], my Lady, ERESHKIGAL, [. . .]. Come, O Storm God of Nerik, my Lord. Wuruntemu [. . .]. May (s)he open [the gates] of the Dark Earth. [. . . he hurried(?)] on account of the bloody, murderous [humanity. The Storm God of Nerik(?)] was afraid of the deity. . . . From Nerik, [from] the honored house, from the *dahangas*-room he went forth. [He went] down to the shores of the Nine Seas. He went down to the banks of the Noble River.[8] Wuruntemu [. . .] covers(?) the tables with a cloth. May the *surasuras*-bird [come] to call an omen for her."

§8 (rev. 7–10) "[May they] tell [it] to the Sun God of the Sky. The son of the Sun Goddess of Arinna [has gone] from mankind. He [. . . ed] to the sea. The Storm God with a loyal heart [came(?)] down from the sky. The Storm God ordained mankind for destruction [. . .]. He summoned Wuruntemu (and) the [Marassanta River]."

§9 (rev. 11–17) "You, O Marassanta River, are close to the soul of the Storm God of Nerik." The Marassanta River once flowed astray(?), but the Storm God turned it and made it flow toward the Sun God of the Gods. He made [it] flow near Nerik. The Storm God said to the Marassanta River: "If someone angers the Storm God of Nerik, and he goes forth from Nerik, from the *dahangas*-room, you, O Marassanta River, must not let him go to another river (or) another spring."

§10 (rev. 18–24) The Storm God of the Sky said to the Marassanta River: "May you be under oath. May you not alter (your) flow." So the Marassanta River did not alter (its) flow. You gods did it. May the Nakkiliyata River evoke the Storm God of Nerik. [May it bring] him from down in the sea, from under the [waves(?)]. May it bring him from down by the Nine (Sea)shores. May it bring [him] from the bank of the Nakkiliyata River. . . .

[*After a damaged section, the text continues with a prayer on behalf of the royal family and the land of Hatti.*]

═══════ 5. Myths of Lost Storm Gods ═══════

a. The Storm God, the Personal God
of Queen Asmunikal

Anger and Disappearance of the God

§1 (A i 5–6) [*Beginning of the text broken away.*] . . . steps before the deity and speaks as follows:

§2 (A i 7–14) "[The Storm God of] Queen Asmunikal became angry. [He drew his . . . backward, and drew] his [. . .] forward. [He put his right] shoe on his left foot. He turned himself around and [went] forth. Mist seized the windows. Smoke [seized] the roof beams. [. . .] became stifled at the altars; [. . .] became stifled [at the . . . ; the . . .] became stifled [at the . . .].

§3 (B 6–11) [The . . . s] turned [. . .] the hearth [. . .] upon it the logs [were stifled]. In the courtyard the sheep [were stifled]. In the cattle barn the cattle [were stifled]. They eat, but they [do] not [become satisfied. They drink, but do not] quench their thirst.

[*Break of undetermined length.*]

Return of the Appeased God

§4 (A iii 1–8) [. . .] sat down on a wooden. . . . The altar [became right again; above it] the gods became right again. [. . .] On the hearth the logs [became right again. In the sheep pen] the sheep became right again. [In] the cattle barn [the cattle became right again]. They eat and [become satisfied]. They drink again [and quench their thirst].

§5 (A iii 9–21) In front of the altar [a hunting bag] of sheepskin [is suspended]. Inside it [lies] The Gentle [Message] of the Lamb. So may there be [in the same way a Gentle] Message for the king and queen before the Personal Storm God (literally, "Storm God of the Head"). Also [inside it] lies [The Right Shank]. *Galaktar* [and *parhuenas-*]plants also lie inside. May The Right Shank also [. . .] before the Personal Storm God. [May it stand] before him. . . . [And as] *galaktar* is lying [in the bag], so you [. . .] be pacified to him. As *parhuenas* [is lying there], so (the god) [should be] invoked to her (i.e., the queen?). (The god) [should give to the king] and to (Queen) Asmunikal sons, daughters, [descendants of the second and third generation], and long [years].

[*Break of undetermined length.*]

b. The Storm God of Queen Harapsili

[*The beginning is broken away.*]

§1 (A ii 12) [. . .] long years [. . .].

§2 (A ii 14–16) [You, O hawthorn tree, wear] white in spring, [but red in the fall]. A sheep [goes out from under you, and you pull out its] wool.

§3 (A iii 1–4) [The Storm God of Queen Harapsili(?)] sat down on a wooden *sarpas*-chair. [. . .]. The mist released [the window]. [The smoke] released [the house]. The altar was in harmony again. [Above it] the gods were in harmony.

§4 (A iii 5–16) [The hearth was in harmony]. Upon it the logs were in harmony. In the courtyard the sheep were in harmony. [In the] cattle [barn] the oxen were in harmony. They ate and once more had enough. They drank and once more had enough. Before [the altar] a hunting bag (made) of a lamb's (fleece) is hanging. In it lies The Gentle Message of the Lamb. In the same way may Queen [Harapsili] be a Gentle Message to the Storm God of Harapsili. In it [lie *galaktar* and] *parhuenas*-plants. [. . .]

§5 (C 1–2) *parhuenas* [lies here. May it . . .] for him (the Storm God of Harapsili).

§6 (C 3–5) [O Storm God, give sons and daughters], grandchildren [and great-grandchildren, and long] years to her.

[*A few traces of two paragraphs, then a break of unknown length.*]

§7 (D 5–9) [. . .] . . . Storm God of Harapsili [. . .] I have [. . . ed to you] rivers of *tawal*- and *walhi*-drink. There lies before you [. . .]. So turn back and [. . .].

§8 (D 10–17) [Look upon] your [. . .] with kindly eyes. [Give her sons] and daughters, . . . [. . . The Storm God] of Harapsili [sat down on a *sarpas*-chair]. He turned [his. . . . The mist released] the windows. The altar was in harmony. [Upon it the gods were in harmony. The hearth was in harmony. Upon it] the [logs were in harmony. In the courtyard the sheep were in harmony. In the cattle barn] the oxen [were in harmony. . . .]

[*End of the text broken away.*]

============ **6. Telipinu and the Daughter of the Sea God** ============

§1 (A i 1–4) Long ago, when the great Sea [. . . ed], heaven, earth, (and) mankind [. . . ed]. The Sea God quarreled and brought [the Sun God] down [from heaven] and [hid] him.

§2 (A i 5–8) In the land (conditions) were bad, and it was dark. But no one could withstand the Sea. [The Storm God called Telipinu], his favorite and firstborn [son].

§3 (A i 9–10) "Come now, Telipinu, you yourself go [. . .] to the Sea. Bring the Sun God of the Sky back from the Sea."

§4 (A ii 11–15) Telipinu went to the Sea. [The Sea] became afraid of him, so that [he gave] him [his] daughter. He also gave the Sun God to him. So Telipinu [brought] back from the Sea [the Sun God] and the daughter of the Sea, and the Storm God [kept] them with himself.

§5 (A ii 16–21) The Sea sent to the Storm God: "Telipinu, your son, [took] my daughter as his wife and took her away. [So what] (bride-price) will you give to me?" The Storm God said to Hannahanna: "A river(?) came from the Sea. He kept demanding [the bride-price(?)]. Shall I give it to him, or shall I not give (it) to him?"

§6 (A ii 22–25) Hannahanna (said) to the Storm God: "Give (it) to him. [Telipinu(?)] took [the Sea's daughter] hither for brideship. . . . [. . .]" So (the Storm God) gave to him a thousand of each: he gave [him one] thousand cattle (and) one thousand sheep. And [he accepted them].

§7 (A ii 26) [. . .] his brothers [. . .].

[*The rest of column ii in A is broken away. Parts of ten lines of B iv give the materials, largely foodstuffs, for a ritual to be performed in connection with the story, just as is the case in Texts 1 and 2.*]

========== 7. The Disappearance of the Sun God ==========

With the disappearance of the Sun the whole of nature is gripped by the paralyzing force of *hahhimas* "Frost."

[*The beginning of the composition is broken away. After a long lacuna it continues.*]
§1 (A i 1–4) [. . .] my [. . .]. When/If to the Storm God [. . .] the noble Sun God, his son. When/If . . . [. . .], then let your . . . show itself with me.

§2 (A i 5–10) "[If] I seize [the Sun God] and hide him, what can the Storm God do? I/He will [. . .]." When they began to praise themselves, the daughter of the Sea God called from [the sky], and the Sea God heard her. Then the Sea God placed a *KUKUBU*-vessel [. . .] on his/its . . . , (saying): "Now, whenever the Sun God falls, (if) he falls in [. . .], or flame, or tree, or bush, [. . .] will be caught in a net(?)."

§3 (A i 11–17) The Sea God says to the Sun God: "This is what [I placed . . .] for you." The Sun God went to the Sea God into his chamber and covered them, (namely?) the *KUKUBU*-vessel(s) [. . .], with wax. Then he stopped (them) up on top (with?) copper, and said: "Keep on praising yourselves until [. . .]. But the Sea God [heard] the words of his daughter. [This] lovely woman [asked(?)] the Storm God: [" . . .] what miracle [will they] make?"

§4 (B i 2–11) [. . .] your sons [. . .]. The Storm God said to the wife [of . . .]: "Tell me: [. . . and . . . are] my sons. If a man has been killed, [can they restore him to life? If] an ox (or) sheep has been killed, can they restore it to life? Then what miracle can your sons (hope to) do? Frost has paralyzed the entire land. He has dried up the waters. Frost is great." (Then the Storm God) says to his brother, the Wind: "The waters of the mountains, the gardens, the meadow(s)—let your refreshing go (through) the lands—but let him (i.e., Frost) not paralyze them."

§5 (B i 12–20) "[He] paralyzed the herbs, the lands, the cattle, the sheep, the dogs, (and) the pigs. But he won't paralyze the crops (which are) 'sons of the heart.' If he (tries to) paralyze them, the fat will hold them inside, so that he will not paralyze them, when [he paralyzes] each and every (thing)." He proceeded to say to the Storm God: "Why has this happened?" Frost says to his father and mother: "You eat and drink this, but you have taken account of nothing. The shepherd and cowherd [have died(?)]." He paralyzed the land, but the Storm God doesn't even know.

§6 (B i 21–31) The Storm God sent for the Sun God, (saying:) "Go bring [*plural*] the Sun God." They went. They search for the Sun God, but they [do] not find him. And the Storm God says: "So why have you not found him? My own body parts have become warm! Where could he have gotten lost?" So he sent the War God, (saying:) "Go bring the Sun God." But Frost seized the War God. (Then the Storm God says:) "Go call [*plural*] the Tutelary Deity. Will (Frost) paralyze him too? Is he not a child of the steppe?" But Frost seized him too. (Then the Storm God says:) "Go call Telipinu. That son of mine is mighty: he breaks up the ground, plows, irrigates, (and) . . . s grain." But Frost holds him too.

§7 (B i 32–41) (Then the Storm God says:) "[Go] call Gulsa and Hanna-hanna. If those have died, [then] these too may have died (i.e., the unborn, which constitute the future of the land). [Did] Frost [come] to their gate too?" Frost says to the Storm God: "[Because(?)] you kill and cast away, all have died. And you no longer hold this same cup." Hasamili's (full) brothers are (Frost's) half brothers. So Frost did not seize them. [Therefore the Storm God(?)] called them. The Storm God speaks(?) to Frost: "My hand is stuck to the cup; [my feet] too they have caused to get stuck. (Even) if [you seize] these feet and hands, do not seize my eyes too."

§8 (B i 42–45) [Frost] speaks to the Storm God: "You will look at your children [. . .]. I will go up to the sky. [. . .] Save [. . . 's hands and] feet. [*The remainder of column i is broken away.*]

§9 (A iv 1–4) [. . .] turned/sent. And he shot(?) the Moon God. [. . .] he threw [. . .] in the city gate. The old men and women [. . .]. And I am an . . . woman.

§10 (A iv 5–7) I . . . ed [on the] left(?) . . . And I did not take it. On the right I . . . ed [. . .], and I took the gods' words. And I poured them out [. . .]. My mouth (and) my . . . [. . .]. And I placed the . . . on top.

§11 (A iv 8–12) I lost none of the gods' words. But whenever Telipinu is difficult toward anyone, I speak the gods' words and invoke him. And the Sun God says: "Let the gods' words go. And my allocation is. . . ." Hanna-hanna says: "And if you, O Sun God, give good to someone, may he give you nine (sacrificial animals). And may the poor man give you one sheep."

§12 (A iv 13) The (text) of the invocation of the Sun God and Telipinu is finished.

8. The Disappearance of Hannahanna

a. Incantation and Distress

[*The beginning of the text is broken away.*]

§1 (A ii 2-4) [Let not the anger, wrath], sin, [and sullenness of Hannahanna go into the fruitful field], grove, or vineyard. Let them go the way of the Dark Earth.

§2 (A ii 5-7) [In the Dark Earth bronze] *palhi*-vessels are lying. [Their lids are of lead.] What goes into them [doesn't] come [back up again]. It perishes therein.

§3 (A ii 8-9) Hannahanna's [anger], wrath, sin, and sullenness [should go into them] and perish therein.

§4 (A ii 10-12) Just as water doesn't flow back up the pipe, let Hannahanna's anger, wrath, sin, and sullenness not come back.

§5 (A ii 13-17) You are the hawthorn tree. In spring you wear white (blossoms), but in harvest season you wear red (ones). The cow goes out from under you, and you pull off a tuft of its hair. The sheep goes out from under you, and you pull off some of its form (i.e., its tufts of wool).

§6 (A ii 18-19) Pull off from Hannahanna her anger, wrath, sin, [and sullenness] too.

§7 (B 4-6) Hannahanna [went off, and mist held] the windows. Smoke held the house. [In the hearth the logs were stifled.] At the altars [the gods] were stifled.

§8 (B 7-11) In the cattle barn the cattle [were stifled. In the sheep pen the sheep] were stifled. [Mothers took no account of their children.] Cows [took no account of] their calves. [Sheep took no account of their lambs.] Hannahanna, rejoicing(?), [came back into the land of Hatti, and came back into her house]. [*The remainder of the text is broken away.*]

b. The Appeasement of the Goddess

[*Beginning is broken away.*]

§9 (A iii? 3-7) [Here is] The Right Shank [for you, (Hannahanna)]. Just as [The Right Shank stands] . . . , may you stand . . . like The Right Shank [to the king] and queen, the princes, and the land of Hatti.

§10 (A iii? 8-13) Hannahanna's soul is stifled like (smoldering) brushwood. Just as they ignite (this) brushwood, and it gives light in the four corners (of the house), may it be light also to your soul and essence, O Hannahanna.

§11 (A iii? 14–16) And just as [this brushwood] burns up, may [Hanna-hanna's] anger, wrath, sin, [and sullenness] also burn up.

§12 (A iii? 17–22) [Hapantali brought] *karsani*-wood from the mountain, and set fire to it in the hearth. Hapantali brought [. . .] from the uncultivated land and poured/scattered it [in . . .] they took their seats and they [. . .] like the [. . .].

§13 (A iii? 23–29) [He/she brought] the holy water of the Queen of the Spring and poured it out on top. A cloud rose. The vapor(?) came up [to the . . .]. It went into Hannahanna's body. It drove from her body [Hanna-hanna's] anger, wrath, [sin, and sullenness]. [*The rest is broken away.*]

===================== 9. Myths of the Goddess Inara =====================

a. A Mission of the Bee (cf. below in d)

§1 [*Column i and part of column ii are broken away.*] (A ii 1–5) [. . .] why [. . .] a rock [. . .]. Now what miracle [can they perform? . . .] the goddess Hannahanna [. . .] the bee.

§2 (A ii 6–10) For three days [. . .] drove. [. . . said:] "I will go to my mother. A spear [. . .]. An *iskarkan*-stone to me. . . . Let me not go near their . . . , that I should lead it/him before the deity [. . .]."

§3 (B ii 4–9) Hannahanna sent a bee to the Tutelary Deity, (saying): "Take a goat's horn and make a sound." The Tutelary Deity made a sound.[6] And everyone went somewhere. The War God heard and feared it. He took with spear and knife, and he made a [. . .] for the Female Attendant. And he went. But no one found humans, cattle, [or sheep].

§4 (B ii 10–17) Hannahanna opened the windows. [. . .] "I see him. The Female Attendant [. . .], the herdsmen of cattle and sheep. . . . The [. . .] men [. . .], but (s)he found nothing. [. . .] (S)he killed the farmers, the cattle, [and the sheep . . .] took rocks [. . .] drove back here [. . .] not. This [. . .]."

[*After traces of two paragraphs the tablet is broken away.*]

b. The Search for a Hunting Bag

[*The beginning of the text is broken away.*]

§1 (ii 1) [. . .] Hannahanna [. . .].

§2 (ii 2–7) I will go to your place [. . .] a hunting bag quietly [. . .] brought. A . . . [. . .] Hannahanna [. . .] the Female Attendant [. . .] [*Column ii breaks off. First part of column iii broken away.*]

§3 (iii 1–2) [. . .] If [. . .] him, then take [. . .] and bring it. But if he [. . .].

§4 (iii 3–9) Don't bring it in here. In front [. . . (Someone)] and he will make [. . .] behind his/its hunting bag. The bee went and brought the hunting bag. While it was coming, Hannahanna made three *wattaru*-basins(?). Over one an *ippiyas*-tree is standing; under the second a wooden *hupparas*-vessel is lying; and in/on the third a fire is burning.

§5 (iii 10–13) Hannahanna sits (there) and looks toward (them). The bee came and placed the hunting bag on/in the wooden *hupparas*-vessel. The deity Miyatanzipa came and sat down under the *ippiyas*-tree.

§6 (iii 14–16) . . . says: "Very good . . . " [. . .] they [. . . ed]. The wooden *hupparas*-vessel [. . .] they [. . . ed].

[*The last portion of column iii and the beginning of iv are broken away. The few parts of lines that are preserved of column iv mention the bee, Hannahanna, and twice the verb "they conceived."*]

c. The Storm God Searches for Inara

§1 (ii 1–5) Hannahanna says to the goddess Inara: [" . . . "]. And Inara says: "[. . .] a man [. . .], and I didn't. . . . So [I came here(?)] to you." Hanna-hanna replies: "Don't [go anywhere]; remain right here."

§2 (ii 6–10) "I will give you a land. And I will give you a man." The Storm God noticed that Inara was missing. He sent a bee, saying: "You go search for her." So the bee went and found Hannahanna and said to her: "The Storm God has noticed his daughter is missing."

§3 (ii 11–13, iii 1–6) [Hannahanna] took the . . . of every (kind of) wild animal and dropped [them] into the hunting bag. And on top she placed [. . .]. Then Hannahanna [. . . ed] the bee. [*End of column ii and beginning of iii broken. The bee seems to be talking to Hannahanna in what follows.*] Let him/her take [. . .] back [. . .] says [. . . the hunter] will not be able to kill [. . .].

§4 (iii 7–9) [*Hannahanna speaks to the bee:*] [. . .] you say; [. . .] respect/importance/difficulty [. . .] I will give.

§5 (iii 10–13) [. . .] to whom [. . .] the hunter to the steppe [. . .] go. [. . .] will be able to kill [. . .].

d. A Mission of the Bee (cf. also above under a)

§1 [*Preceding context broken away.*] (2–4) [. . .] Bring [. . .] before [. . .] (s)he will see his/her/its . . . [. . .] didn't find the [. . .].

§2 (5–12) Hannahanna sent the bee, saying: "[You go] search [for her]." The bee went [. . . and found(?)] her (i.e., Inara's?) wagon. And [the . . .] holds her, so that she doesn't want [to come back(?)]. The bee went to Hannahanna [. . .]. And Hannahanna [said: " . . .] Take wax and [. . .] her head."

§3 (13–16) "Now take, and it to/from her [. . .] gather. [You must soothe] (her) form [with the wax(?)]. Under (her) feet [you must . . . her.]" [*End of the readable context.*]

e. Hannahanna and the War God

§1 [*Preceding context broken away.*] (A obv. 1–4) If/When [. . .] him/her [. . .] brought out of the gate [. . .] Hannahanna says.

§2 (A obv. 5–9) He/She went and found the *peru*-stone. [. . .] spoke as follows: "Come, [. . .] become [my(?)] Female Attendant." The stone [. . .] Hannahanna replies: [" . . . "] Hannahanna [. . . ed.]

§3 (A obv. 10) [. . .] her Female Attendant [. . .]. [*Following context lost.*]

§4 [*The following lines are from the reverse of A with restorations from B. Preceding context lost.*] (A rev. 2–5) "When you go before the Sun God, do not again make [. . .] everything. You will go and find [. . .]. You will say [. . .]. When the Sun God says 'You do something,' he says: 'You [. . .].'"

§5 (A rev. 6–10) "But if he says nothing, let him be silent(?)." The War God replied: "But if I do not go anywhere, what shall I take?" Hannahanna replied to him: "Year by year keep going on military campaigns."

§6 (A rev. 11–13) The three children of the Female Attendant [ask] Hannahanna: "Behold, what shall we take?" (Hannahanna replied:) "Go [. . .]! Do not go [. . .]!"

§7 (A rev. 14–16) [The . . . s] said [to . . .]. [*Following context lost.*]

f. The Female Attendant

§1 [*The following lines are from the obverse of A. Preceding context lost.*] . . . [. . .] Just as its lord/owner [. . .] not oxen, not sheep. Like [the . . .], he too in the same way [. . .]. Go ye, and . . . the Female Attendant. [Now . . .] stood before the gate. [. . .]. "Come, [. . .] birds, together with cattle and sheep [. . .] the Female Attendant [. . .] you [*singular*] will go, and [. . .]."

§2 [*Preceding context lost.*] (B obv. 1–3) [. . .] struck [. . .].

§3 (B obv. 4–7) [. . .] it too will become blunt. [. . .] with the sistrum(?) [. . . and] it too will become blunt. [. . .] didn't find [. . .].

§4 (B obv. 8–14) [. . .] on the rock/cliff [. . .] her Female Attendant [. . .] not [. . .] you will carry off [. . .] they [. . . ed]. The child [. . .] Hannahanna [. . .]. [*Following context lost.*]

§5 [*The following lines are from the reverse of A with restorations from B. Preceding context lost.*] (1–10) [. . .] one last [. . .] slaughter. So go. If they ask any question, only (s)he will notice you, saying: "(S)he will go cradle(?) me. Bring [. . .] to me. You spoke some sign/miracle [. . .]". Hannahanna said: "What shall I say to you? Did Inara make no sound at all? You [surely] heard [. . .], and [. . .]" [. . .] leaped, and [. . .] destroyed the city of the Female Attendant.

[*Following context broken away.*]

========= **10. Kamrusepa Myths** =========

This selection is taken from column iv, which is well preserved. There are ends of lines in earlier columns. Of these it is especially in column i that we see signs of mythological material.

§1 (iv 1–2) Kamrusepa looked (down) from heaven. [. . .] she recounts (the story) in the same way.

§2 (iv 3–6) Thus says Kamrusepa: "Go take the fire of the steppe. Take the wheat of irrigation. Take red, black, and green wool. Take the stalk(?) of the reed/arrow. Enchant it/them and wind [this one] on his neck, but that one on his feet.

§3 (iv 7–10) "And let the illness of his head become a mist, and let it ascend to heaven. Let the Dark Earth lift his illness with the hand. The cloud will not overcome the illness. Up above, let heaven overcome it. Below, let the Dark Earth overcome it." This is the spell of the fire.

§4 (iv 11–14) They gave. They gave to it (i.e., to the fire) the grain (disease?). They gave illness to it. They gave the eye illness to it. They gave the foot illness to it. They gave the hand illness to it. They gave the head illness to it. And (its) heat vanished, so that it wails.

§5 (iv 15–19) The Sea God questions it: "So why are you going about wailing?" (The fire answers:) "The heat in my crock [has vanished]. [. . .] Shall we take it from someone? The evil. . . . Let him dress himself in dark clothing, and [. . .], and [let him go] to heaven on the staircase/ladder with nine steps."

§6 (iv 20–26) So he takes his stand before Mother Kamrusepa (and says:) "The heat has vanished from [my] crock." Kamrusepa (replies): "Shall we take [it] from someone?" They led him [secretly(?)] to the river, and before the heat they pierced it with a shepherd's crook, and they held it [out], so that the river glowed. They [held] it out, so that [the . . .] glowed.

§7 (iv 27–35) They hold the meadow [. . .], and the meadow burns [. . .]. They hold the mountains [. . .], so that the mountains burn [. . .]. She joined(?) [. . .] through the midst of the meadow(?), so that [. . . the . . .] . . . heat, and it (i.e., the fire) [before] him/her [no longer] wails. The wheat [. . . And . . .] looked out of the window. [He saw . . .] the mountains(?). He took a sinew [of . . .] of the ruined house [. . .].

[*The rest of the text is broken away.*]

========= **11. The Voyage of the Immortal Human Soul** =========

§1 (i 1–15) [. . .] The ox . . . s. The sheep [. . . s. . . .] The sky . . . s. [. . .] . . . [. . .] the human soul [. . .] came. If it is in the mountain, let the bee bring it and put it in its place. If, however, it is in the plain, let the bee (again) bring it and put it in its place. That which is from the plowed field, let the bees bring and put it in its place. Let the bees go a journey of three (or) four days and bring my . . . here. If it is in the direction of the sea, let the *lahanza*-duck bring it and put it in its place. If, however, it is in the direction of the river, let the *huwalas*-bird bring it and put it in its place.

§2 (i 16–25) And what is from the sky, let the eagle . . . bring it in its talons. Let the desired thing/one be struck by their talons. Let the goat(?) strike with its hoof(?). Let the sheep strike with its horns. Let the mother sheep strike with its nose(?). The Mother Goddess(?) is tearful. She is struck with tears. What things are dear to her are "opened" upon the eight body parts. Let her be struck (with regard to) them. The soul is luxuriant/thriving and [. . .]. Let nothing be impossible for it.

§3 (i 26–37) The soul is great. The soul is great. Whose soul is great? The mortal soul is great. And what road does it travel? It travels the invisible road. The traveler has fit it for himself for this road. A holy thing is the soul of the Sun Goddess, the soul of the Mother. Why must I, a mortal, go into the pit(?)? I would rather go into the. . . . I would rather fall into the river. [I would rather fall] into the pond. I would rather go into the *tenawas*. [. . .] the *tenawas* is evil [. . . let not . . . go(?)] to the meadow [. . .] to the god [. . .].

[*The rest of the text is broken away. It is possible that the following fragment belongs somewhere in this lacuna.*[7]]

§4 (ii 2–10, iii 1–7) [. . .] The evil *tenawas* [holds(?) him(?), so that] he does not recognize [them]. One doesn't recognize the other. Sisters having the same mother do [not] recognize (each other). Brothers having the same father do [not] recognize (each other). A mother does [not] recognize [her] own child. [A child] does [not] recognize [its own] mother. [. . .] does [not] recognize [. . .] . . . [. . .] does [not] recognize [. . .]. (iii 1) From a fine table they do not eat. From a fine stool they do not eat. From a fine cup they do not drink. They do not eat good food. They do not drink my good drink. They eat bits of mud. They drink waste waters(?).

§5 (iii 8–11) Emaciation(?) [. . .]. Upon them [. . .]. And the father [. . .] dried [up(?) . . .].

12. When the Storm God Thunders Frightfully
(Also known as: "The Moon that Fell from Heaven")

This myth is preserved in a bilingual version. The original Hattic language version is in the left-hand column; the Hittite translation is in the right-hand column. Since the Hattic language is still poorly understood, this translation is based on the Hittite translation.

a. Introduction

Version A

§1 (1–4) [When the Storm God] thunders frightfully, (the Man of the Storm God) [takes] the following: two bulls, two [. . . s], one copper [. . .], one copper knife, one copper axe, red, white, and black wool, of each a loop.

§2 (5–7) When they have assembled all this, they [. . .] the Man [of the Storm God]. The Man of the Storm God takes fifty thick breads, [a selection(?)] of pegs: [. . .] pegs of silver and bronze, and a peg of cornel wood, and [he . . . s them . . .].

Version B = C

§3 (B 1–2 = C 1–2) [When] the Storm God thunders frightfully, [. . .] frightens(?) [. . .] And the Man of the Storm God [. . . s] to [. . .].

§4 (B 3–5 = C 4–6) And he takes this: one ox, five sheep, [. . . , . . .] dipping vessels for *tawal*-drink, two . . . , nine thick breads of one half *UPNU*-measure (of flour), one half [. . .] of a *hazzilas*-measure (of flour), two warm loaves, one cheese, one rennet, one *UPNU*-measure of fruit, one *NAMMANTU*-vessel of honey, one *putis*-measure of salt.

§5 (B 6–8 = C 7–8) And the Man of the Storm God appears daily facing the Storm God. He [takes/holds . . .] and one thick bread, one *KUKUBU*-vessel of wine and one *KUKUBU*-vessel of sweet milk. And when the Storm God thunders, [. . . s]. The Man of the Storm God breaks one thick bread, pours a libation of sweet milk, and speaks as follows in the Hattic language.

b. The Myth

§6 (C ii 10–14) [The Moon God] fell from the sky and fell upon the gate complex, [but] no one saw him. The Storm God [sent] rain after him; he sent rains after him. Fear seized him; anxiety seized him.

§7 (C ii 15–16) The god Hapantali went there. He stood [beside him] and uttered over him the words of a spell.

§8 (A ii 15–17) The goddess Kamrusepa looked down from the sky (and said:) "What in the world [has happened(?)] here? The Moon God fell from the sky and fell upon the gate complex."

§9 (A ii 19–21) The Storm God saw him and sent rains after him; he sent rains after him. Fear seized him; anxiety seized him.

§10 (A ii 22–23) Hapantali went there. He stood beside him and uttered over him the words of a spell.

§11 (A ii 25–26) What will you proceed to do? Kamrusepa will send after him. So I will go to Mount [. . .] and release [. . .] from the rock.

§12 (A ii 27–29) Let it/him bark, or let it/him. . . . Then let them go, and let the fears and anxieties remain . . . ing inside [the . . .].

§13 (A ii 30–33) [The] sky [opened/bore]. And he made (it). And he became frightened. [. . .] became frightened. The Storm God opened/bore. And he made (it). [And he became frightened.] Labarna the king with his mind [. . .] Labarna the king [. . .].

c. The Ritual

Most of what is preserved is in a poor state and hardly merits translation. I give here one better-preserved section. The strange expression "he drinks two oxen, etc." alludes to a procedure of naming cups of beverage after deities, etc. To drink the contents of that cup is to drink the object or being whose name it bears.

A iii = C iii

§14 (C iii 3–5) [Next he drinks two] oxen, a wagon, [a spear], the [weapon] of the Storm God three times. He breaks [three] thick loaves.

§15 (C iii 6–9) [Next while standing] he drinks the Thunders and [Lightnings], the clouds, the rains [of the Storm God three] times. He breaks [three thick loaves].

§16 (C iii 10–16) [Next] he drinks the Fears and Anxieties of the Storm God nine times. He breaks [nine] thick loaves. All the while the Man of the Storm God is drinking this cup no one is permitted to make a sound; it is forbidden. Then he places them (i.e., the cups?) in the gate separately.

§17 (A iii 17–19) Next while standing he drinks the Divine Heptad of the Storm God one time. He breaks eleven thick loaves.

§18 (A iii 20–21) Then the Man of the Storm God goes back home to his house and makes a libation [before] the Storm God of the Sky.

§19 (Colophon) Tablet one, finished, (of the text entitled) "When [the Storm God] thunders frightfully, the Man of the Storm God does as follows."

13. Fragments of Myths about Lost and Found Deities

a. The Anger of a God, Distress, and Mission of the Eagle

§1 [*Beginning broken away.*] (A 2) [. . .] then he speaks as follows:

§2 (A3–B2) [. . . (such-and-such a god)] became angry, and [. . . ed . . .] He put [his right shoe] on his [left foot]. [The] smoke(?) seized his eyes [. . .]. At the altars [. . . seized]. And their eyes [. . . In the sheepfold] it seized(?) the sheep. In the [cattle barn it seized the cattle]. They drink, [but they cannot quench their thirst.]

§3 (B 3–8) The Sun God [made] a feast [and] summoned the gods. The Sun God [looked for . . . 's] eyes, but he could not find [them] there. So the Sun God [summoned the other gods(?) and said:] "Go [summon] the swift eagle for me." They went and [summoned] the swift eagle. [The Sun God said to] the eagle: ["Go] search [. . .]." [*Following context lost.*]

b. Missions of the Eagle and the Bee

§1 [*Preceding context broken away.*] (ii 4–8) [. . .] "Search [. . .] the waves(?) [. . .] search. Search the [springs] surrounded by *ippiyas*-trees. Search the forest(s)."

§2 (ii 9–20) [. . .] the thunder(?). [The eagle] went, [but] it did not find [the . . .]; it did not find [. . .]. It searched the [. . . s]; it searched the long roads. It searched [the . . .]. Then the eagle [. . . ed to . . . , and said: "I searched] the rushing streams(?). I searched [the . . .]s, but I didn't find (him). I searched [the . . .], but I didn't find (him). I searched [the . . .], but I didn't find (him). [I spied out(?)] the standing [. . .]s. I searched the springs surrounded by *ippiyas*-trees. I searched [the . . .], but I didn't find (him). I searched [the . . .]. I searched the good forest."

§3 (ii 21–28) "[O] . . . (?) [bee], you hold honey in your heart. [So] you should [search] the high mountains." [The eagle(?)] makes the circuit of all the places, (saying:) "I have searched [all the] places. In the good forests [I didn't] find (him). Is he going to Hattusa [. . .] to the vineyard(s)? Will he lie down [on the . . . ?] Will he [lie] down on [the . . . ? Will he lie] down on [the . . . ? Will he lie] down in the moor/thicket? [Will he go] down into the [Dark Earth? . . .] [*Following context is only traces and the rest is lost.*]

c. Search for the Fate Goddesses
and Mother Goddesses

[*Preceding context lost.*] (A ii 1–13) [. . .] says [. . .] the Fate Goddesses and the Mother Goddesses; [. . .]. They [. . .]ed for themselves meadows, [. . .] feet with underbrush [. . .]. They [. . .] away the hairs from mud(?) [. . . They . . .] the eyes [. . .]. The weighty gods searched for them. They searched the high mountains but did not find him. They searched the flowing [rivers], but did [not] find [him]. They searched the holy . . . s but did not find [him]. They turned [. . .] forth. They found [. . .] in the forest. They found [. . .] in the [. . .]. [*Following context lost.*]

d. Ritual to Appease the Deity

§1 [*Preceding context lost.*] (A iii 2–4) [. . . In the same way let them . . .] to [the king, the queen, the princes, and princesses, to the second] and third [generations].

§2 (A iii 5–9) Behold here lies [*samama*-nuts and. . . . As *samama*-nuts are . . . , as] raisins [hold wine within them], as olives [hold oil within them, so may the Storm God] and the Sun Goddess of Arinna [likewise be . . .].

§3 (A iii 10–15) As this cheese [. . .] is fine, [as . . . is bright, and . . .] food and drink [. . .] so may [the . . .] be likewise fine to the king, queen, [princes, and princesses] and may it be bright.

§4 (A iii 16–19) He places liver before [the god . . . and says:] "You, O god, eat! [And] give [to the king a propitious(?)] liver omen, [and turn] everything favorable for the king and queen. [. . .]" [*Following context broken away.*]

Notes

1. In these broken lines some would see an account of Inara's killing Hupasiya. But although this is possible, there is no clear evidence for his death. In any case, from this point on Hupasiya disappears from the story, which could mean either that he died or was sent home.

2. Or: Zaliyanu asked for rain.

3. *ANET,* 190, §36.

4. This and the following items that lie inside the hunting bag are probably symbols of what the worshipers want from the gods.

5. After the eagle's failure, version 1 told of a search by the Storm God. But this incident is omitted in version 2.

6. Variant adds: "and they . . . ed to help."

7. This fragment, like §3 of the main text, mentions the "evil *tenawas*" as a kind of prelude to the existence of the soul in the afterlife. Although it has not been proved that it belongs to the same text, it seems very likely.

8. Comparison of §7 with §10 shows that the "Noble River" is the Nakkiliyat River.

II

Hurrian Myths

Introduction

The most important group of myths in the Hittite language is the Kumarbi Cycle. The earliest Kumarbi myths to be edited were the Song of Kumarbi and the Song of Ullikummi (Forrer 1936; Güterbock 1946). Both were translated into English by Goetze (1955). A definitive edition of Ullikummi was prepared by Güterbock (1961). Until 1971, as can be seen both from Güterbock 1961 and Laroche 1971, only three fairly well-preserved compositions were attributed to this cycle: what was termed the Kingship of LAMMA (Text 15), the Theogony, or Kingship in Heaven (Text 14) and the Song of Ullikummi (Text 18). Laroche (1971) identified further fragments which he thought belonged to this cycle. Siegelová (1971) demonstrated by means of new fragments, as well as new supplements to previously known pieces, that the so-called Hedammu myth (Text 17) also belonged to the Kumarbi Cycle.

Hoffner (1988b) reconstructed the myth about the personified Silver (Text 16), demonstrating that this story too was a "song" belonging to the Kumarbi series. We know from colophons that in the native terminology Text 18 was called the Song of Ullikummi, and Text 14 the Song of Ku[marbi]. The Silver myth's proemium contains the statement *ishamihhi* "I sing," which shows it to be the Song of Silver. Hence, all parts of the Kumarbi Cycle without preserved colophons probably bore the names "Song of So-and-So" with the relevant name drawn from the central character in the piece. Most likely the scribes called Text 15 the Song of LAMMA, Text 17 the Song of Hedammu, and Text 16 the Song of Silver.[1]

The sequence of the stories is uncertain. It was always assumed that the Song of Kumarbi (Text 14) contains the beginning. This assumption has now been strengthened by Hoffner. He argued that only the Song of Kumarbi opened with a call to all the gods to hear the tale. All subsequent songs in the cycle opened, as do Silver and Ullikummi, with a description of a powerful adversary of Tessub whose name is given only at the end of the proem in the words "I am singing of So-and-So." Clues in the plots of the individual stories argue for the sequence: Song of Kumarbi, Song of LAMMA, Song of Silver, Song of Hedammu, and Song of Ullikummi.

The central theme of the entire cycle is the competition between Kumarbi and Tessub for kingship over the gods. As pointed out by Hoffner (1975:136–45), the sequence of divine rulers in the Song of Kumarbi is not a father, son, grandson, but an alternation of two competing lines. Alalu, driven from his throne by Anu, is the father of Kumarbi, who in turn drives Anu from his throne. Furthermore, when Kumarbi emasculates Anu to forestall his own removal by any descendant of Anu, he inadvertently makes his own belly the womb for Anu's seed, which produces Tessub, Tasmisu, the Tigris River (Hurrian name Aranzah), and several other gods. Although the end of the Song of Kumarbi is lost, everyone agrees that, since the Song of Ullikummi finds Tessub as king of the gods, he may have already attained that position by the end of the Song of Kumarbi. What has emerged from the recent reconstructions of Hedammu and Silver (Texts 16 and 18) is that in all subsequent songs of the cycle Kumarbi seeks to depose Tessub by means of some offspring of his own. Ullikummi is Kumarbi's son by sexual union with a huge cliff. Hedammu is probably his son[2] by Sertapsuruhi, the daughter of the Sea God. Silver is his son by a mortal woman. It is not clear in what relationship the god LAMMA stands to Kumarbi. At one point we learn that Ea and Kumarbi had agreed to make him king of the gods. Certainly nothing excludes his being Kumarbi's son.

The two antagonists, Kumarbi and Tessub, are from opposite spheres. Kumarbi is a netherworld god, whereas Tessub is a celestial god. In the Song of Kumarbi (Text 14), Kumarbi's father Alalu is driven from the throne by Anu and takes refuge from Anu in the netherworld (the "Dark Earth"). Later, when Anu flees from Kumarbi, he heads for the sky.

When one assembles a list of the deities in these myths who give allegiance to one side or the other, the opposition of netherworld and sky is confirmed. In Kumarbi's camp are Alalu, Kumarbi's vizier Mukisanu, the Great Sea God, the Sea God's vizier Impaluri, the Sea God's daughter Sertapsuruhi, Hedammu, Daganzipa (Earth), Silver, Ullikummi, the Irsirras deities, and probably Ubelluri (who lives under the earth).

In Tessub's camp are Anu, Tasmisu/Suwaliyat, Hebat, Hebat's maidservant Takiti, Sauska/ISHTAR, the divine bulls Seri and Hurri, the Sun and Moon Gods, the War God Astabi, Tessub's brother the Aranzah River (= the Tigris), the Mountain God Kanzura, KA.ZAL, and NAM.HE.

A third group of deities, generally unaligned, includes Ea, Ellil, LAMMA, Kubaba, the Primeval Deities (Nara-Napsara, Minki, Ammunki, Ammezzadu, Ishara, etc.).

According to the proem of the Song of Kumarbi, the entire cycle of songs is addressed to the Primeval Deities. This epithet is sometimes translated "the Former Gods."

Ea, the Mesopotamian god of wisdom, occupies a special position in the developing narrative. In the Song of Kumarbi (Text 14) he assists Kumarbi in ridding himself of the burden of Anu's seed. Toward the end of the Song of Kumarbi Tessub must be cautioned not to curse Ea, because there still was hope that he might be won over from Kumarbi's side. That Tessub was tempted to curse him shows that at this point he was aiding Kumarbi. In the Song of LAMMA, Ea and Kumarbi made LAMMA king (in the place of Tessub?). But by the time of the song of Hedammu, Ea has become troubled by the wasteful destructiveness of the quarrel between Tessub and Kumarbi and he scolds and warns both sides (Text 17, fragment 6, §2). In the Song of Ullikummi (Text 18), which may be the latest "song" of those preserved for us, Ea helps Tessub's allies find the secret of Ullikummi's vulnerability.

The gradual transformation of Ea's loyalty from Kumarbi to Tessub may be one of the few remaining clues to the original sequence of the "songs." A second clue is in the behavior of Sauska. In Hedammu she learns the effectiveness of sexual seduction against the monster Hedammu. But when she tries it again against Ullikummi, it fails because that creature is deaf and blind. This suggests that Hedammu preceded Ulli-kummi in the cycle.

The subsequent use of the Song of Kumarbi by Greek authors (Dirlmeier 1955; Güterbock 1948; Haas 1975; Heubeck 1955; Steiner 1958; Walcot 1966) is interesting in its own right, but is not pertinent to the interpretation of the Hurro-Hittite work.

=========== 14. The Song of Kumarbi ===========

§1 (A i 1-4) . . . who are Primeval Gods, let the [. . .], weighty gods listen: Nara, Napsara, Minki, (and) Ammunki! Let Ammezzadu listen! Let [. . . and . . .], the father and mother of [. . .] listen!

§2 (A i 5-11) Let [. . . and . . .] the father and mother of Ishara, listen! Ellil and NINLIL, who [below] and above (are) weighty, mighty deities, [. . .] and . . . , let them listen! Long ago, in primeval years Alalu was king in heaven. Alalu was sitting on the throne, and weighty Anu, the foremost of the gods, was standing before him. He was bowing down at his (Alalu's) feet, and was placing in his hand the drinking cups.

§3 (A i 12-17) For a mere nine years Alalu was king in heaven. In the ninth year Anu gave battle against Alalu and he defeated Alalu. He (Alalu) fled before him and went down to the Dark Earth. Down he went to the Dark Earth, and Anu took his seat on his throne. Anu was sitting on his throne, and weighty Kumarbi was giving him drink. (Kumarbi) was bowing down at his feet and placing in his hand the drinking cups.

§4 (A i 18-24) For a mere nine years Anu remained king in heaven. In the ninth year Anu gave battle against Kumarbi. Kumarbi, Alalu's offspring, gave battle against Anu. Anu can no longer withstand Kumarbi's eyes. Anu wriggled loose from his (Kumarbi's) hands and fled. He set out for the sky. (But) Kumarbi rushed after him, seized Anu by the feet/legs, and dragged him down from the sky.

§5 (A i 25-29) (Kumarbi) bit his (Anu's) loins, and his "manhood" united with Kumarbi's insides like bronze (results from the union of copper and tin). When Kumarbi had swallowed the "manhood" of Anu, he rejoiced and laughed out loud. Anu turned around and spoke to Kumarbi: "Are you rejoicing within yourself because you have swallowed my 'manhood'?"

§6 (A i 30-36) "Stop rejoicing within yourself! I have placed inside you a burden. First, I have impregnated you with the noble Storm God (=Tessub). Second, I have impregnated you with the irresistible Tigris River. Third, I have impregnated you with the noble Tasmisu. Three terrible gods I have placed inside you as burdens. In the future you will end up striking the boulders of Mount Tassa with your head!"

§7 (A i 37–41) When Anu had finished speaking, he went up to the sky and hid himself. Kumarbi, the wise king, spat from his mouth. He spat from his mouth spittle(?) [and semen] mixed together. What³ Kumarbi spat up, Mount Kanzura [. . . ed] the frightful [. . .].

§8 (A i 42–46) Kumarbi, wailing(?), went to the city of Nippur. He sat down on a lordly [throne]. Kumarbi doesn't [. . .]. (Someone) counts [the months]. The seventh(?) month arrived, and inside of him the mighty [deities . . .].

§9 (A ii 1–3) . . . Kumarbi [*accusative*]. From his . . . from the body come out! Or come out from his mind(?)! Or come out from his good place!

§10 (A ii 4–15) The god A.GILIM (from?) within (Kumarbi's) interior began to speak words to Kumarbi: May you be living, O lord of the source of wisdom! Were I to come out, [. . .] he who [. . .] to Kumarbi . . . which. . . . The Earth will give me her strength(?). The Sky will give me his valor. Anu will give me his manhood. Kumarbi will give me his wisdom. The primeval [. . .] will give [me . . .]. Nara will give me his. . . . And (s)he gave . . . Ellil will give me his strength(?), [. . .] his dignity, and his wisdom. And he gave . . . to all hearts. . . . And . . . of the mind . . . [*Break.*]

§11 (A ii 16–22) Let the stand [. . .] to me. Suwaliyat [. . .]. When/if . . . he gave to me, he [. . .] to me.

§12 (A ii 23–28) Anu began to rejoice(?) . . . come! . . . to you . . . I feared. You will [. . .] and what [. . .]s I gave into [. . .], . . . come! They will . . . him like another woman. Come out in just the same way! . . . . . . come out by the mouth! . . . come out! If you wish, come out by the "good place"!

§13 (A ii 29–38) Ea began to speak [words] to Kumarbi's interior. [. . .] . . . place. If I come [out] to you(?), it will snap me off like a reed. If I come out to you . . . , that too will defile me. . . . it will defile me on the ear. If I come out through the "good place," a . . . woman will . . . me upon my head(?). . . . He . . . ed it within. He split him like a stone. He left him, namely, Kumarbi. The divine KA.ZAL, the valiant king, came up out of his skull.

§14 (A ii 39–54) As he went, KA.ZAL took his stand before Ea and bowed. Kumarbi fell down; from [. . . his . . .] changed (color?). Kumarbi looked for NAM.HE. He began to speak to Ea: "Give me my child, that I may eat him up. What woman to me [. . . s]. I will eat up Tessub. I will smash him like a brittle reed." . . . . . . before . . . . . . Ea . . . he intentionally gathered him. . . . Kumarbi [*accusative*]. . . . The Sun God of the Sky saw him. . . . Kumarbi began to eat. [The Basalt injured(?)] Kumarbi's mouth and teeth. When it had . . . ed in his teeth, Kumarbi began to weep.

§15 (A ii 55–70) Kumarbi [. . . ed]. And words [he began to] speak. Who was I afraid of? Kumarbi . . . like a . . . [. . . ed]. To Kumarbi he began to

speak. Let them call [. . . a . . .] stone! Let it be placed [. . .]! He threw the
Basalt into the [. . .], (saying:) "In the future let them call you [. . .]! Let
the rich men, the valiant lords, slaughter for you cattle [and sheep]! Let the
poor men make sacrifice to you with [meal]!" Not it . . . . . . Because [. . .
. . . ed] Kumarbi from the mouth, no one [will . . .] his [. . .] back. Kumarbi
spoke [. . .]. A . . . occurred to him. . . . they . . . the lands above and below.

§16 (A ii 71–75) [The rich men] began to slaughter with cattle and rams.
[The poor men] began to sacrifice with meal. [The . . . s] began to [. . .].
They closed up(?) his skull like/as (they would mend a torn) garment [. . .].
He (the Storm God) left him, (namely,) Kumarbi. The heroic Tessub came out
through the [good] place.

§17 (A ii 76–86) [. . .] the Fate Goddesses. And [they closed up(?)] his
good place like/as (they would mend a torn) garment. . . . second place [. . .]
. . . [. . .] came out. They (i.e., midwives) brought him to birth [. . .] like
a woman of the bed. When [they had prepared(?)] Kumarbi for (the birth of)
Mount Kanzura, [they brought] him to birth, (namely,) Mount Kanzura.
[And . . .] the hero came (out). [. . .] he came out through the good place.
Anu rejoiced(?) too, [as/because(?)] he beheld [his sons(?)]. [Rest of column ii
broken off.]

§18 (A iii 2–21) [. . .] we will destroy [. . .]. Anu [. . . . . .] Furthermore
we will destroy [. . . also]. [. . .] him in their midst [. . .] we will destroy
NAM.HE like a [. . .]. When [Kumarbi . . . . . .], what words you/he spoke
[. . .], will you destroy Kumarbi [. . .]? [. . .] on my throne [. . .]
Kumarbi [accusative]. Who [will] destroy Tessub for us? And when he comes
to maturity(?), they will make someone else [. . .]. [. . .] will actually/
indeed leave [. . .]. Abandon him! [. . .] Ea, lord of the source of wisdom.
Make [. . .] king! [. . .] word(s) [. . .] . . . [. . .]. When Tessub [heard
these words], he became sad. [Tessub . . .] said to (his) bull, Seri:

§19 (A iii 22–29) "[Who] can come against [me any more] in battle? [Who
can] defeat [me now]? Even Kumarbi [cannot(?)] arise [against me(?)]! Even
Ea [. . .] the son, and the Sun God [. . .]. I drove [Kumarbi(?) from his
throne(?)] at the time [of . . .]. I cursed him [. . .]. I cursed the War God too,
and brought him to the town Banapi. So who now can do battle any more
against me?"

§20 [In what follows Tessub's bull Seri warns him of the danger of cursing certain
other deities and cautions him against overconfidence.] (A iii 30–39) The bull Seri
replied to Tessub: "My lord! Why are you cursing them, [. . . the . . .] gods?
My lord, why [are you cursing] them? Why are you cursing Ea also?"[4] Ea will
hear you [. . .] with. . . . Is it not so? [. . .] (is) great. The mal is as big as
the land. Powerful(?) for you [is . . .]. [. . .] will come. You will not be able
to lift [your(?)] neck(?). [. . .] speaks. [. . .] wise(?) is he. [. . .] Ea. [Break
of about twenty-five lines.]

§21 (A iii 64–66) ". . . of the hand [. . .] May he loose . . . ! [May he . . .]
eyebrows! May he make . . . (of) silver (and) gold!"

§22 (A iii 67–72) When Ea heard the words, he became sad in (his) heart. And he began to speak words back to the god Tauri(?): "Do not speak curses to me! He who cursed me curses me [at great risk to himself(?)]. You who repeat to me [those curses(?)] are yourself cursing me! Under the pot [a fire is placed(?)], and that pot will boil over(?)."[5] [*End of column iii. First fifty lines of column iv broken away. The first preserved lines mention a wagon, which is personified in what follows.*]

§23 (A iv 6–16) When the sixth month passed, the Wagon [. . . . . .] The Wagon's "manhood" [. . . ed] the Wagon back [to . . .] contrived a plan. [. . .] endured(?), Ea, [lord of the source of] wisdom. The Earth Goddess set out for Apzuwa, (saying:) "Ea, [lord of the source of] wisdom, knows what to do." He (Ea?) counts (the months): The first, the second, the third month passed. The fourth, the fifth, the sixth month passed. [The seventh], the eighth, the ninth month passed. And the tenth month [arrived]. In the tenth month the Earth Goddess [began to] cry out in labor pains.

§24 (A iv 17–27) When the Earth cried out in labor pains, [. . .] she bore sons. A messenger went (to tell the king of the gods). And [the god . . . , the king], on his throne approved. [. . .] drove(?) the fine word. [. . .] The Earth has borne two sons/children. [. . . When] Ea [heard] the words, [he . . .] orally(?) a messenger [. . . . And the god . . .], the king, [. . .] a gift.[6] (The king gives) a fine garment for him/her [. . .] an *IPANTU*-garment trimmed with silver for [. . .] wraps [. . .].

§25 (Colophon: A iv 28–35) Tablet one of the Song [of Kumarbi], not complete(?). Written by (literally, "hand of") Ashapa, son of [. . .]tassu, grandson of LAMMA.SUM, ⟨great⟩ grandson of Warsiya, student of Zita. Since the tablet I copied from was worn, I, Ashapa, recopied it under the supervision of (my supervisor) Zita.

15. The Song of the God LAMMA

[*The beginning of the text is broken away. When it begins to be readable, a battle is taking place. Sauska addresses her brother Tessub as "my brother" and "younger brother."*]

§1 (A i 2–12) . . . While Sauska was speaking [to her brother Tessub], the arrow of LAMMA [sped], and it pierced(?) Sauska in her breast. A second arrow of LAMMA [sped]. They (Tessub and Sauska?) hastened the chariot to [. . .], [but LAMMA's arrow] pierced [. . .], so that [. . .] could no longer . . . they could no longer set out.

§2 (A i 13–20) LAMMA forced [. . .]. He took [. . .] and [. . .] it behind Tessub. The stone [went(?)] after Tessub. It struck the sky and shook [out the sky like a garment], so that [Tessub] fell down [from the sky]. LAMMA [. . . ed], and took the reins and the [whip] out of Tessub's hand.

§3 (A i 21–31) Tessub turned back and began to speak [to LAMMA]: "You have taken [my] reins [and whip] from my hand and [taken them into your own] hand. Those reins are sacred(?)! They will summon you to the *kallistar-wa*-house, and the reins [. . .] to you. Let a women not eat of the sheep they sacrifice to the reins. A man [. . . , and . . .] he holds."

[*Text breaks for about thirty or forty lines, which probably told how Ea appointed* LAMMA *to be king of the gods.*]

§4 (A ii 1–7) Now [when] LAMMA [heard] Ea's words, he began to rejoice within himself. [He . . . ed], he ate and drank, and went up to heaven [to kingship(?)]. [. . .] up to heaven [. . .].

§5 (A ii 8–27) [For . . . years] LAMMA was [king] in heaven. And in those years [. . .] wolves [. . .] did not exist. The [. . .] of weaving(?)/woven cloth(?) was striking/crushing [. . .] the BABAZA. [. . . ed the . . .] place, *tawal-* and *walhi*-drink. In the night what [. . .], takes butter, [and the . . .] which he keeps placing [. . .], takes [. . .]. At the gate [. . .]. And he [. . . s] . . . [The mountains(?)] flowed [with] "beer-wine." The valleys [and . . .] flowed [with . . .] poured out. Man [. . . was well off(?)], and he was fully [. . .]. And in what [. . . he . . . ed], there he [. . . ed]. No one began to [. . .] to/for him. In(to) the city of [. . . he . . .]ed. [*The end of column ii is broken away.*]

§6 (A iii 1–18) [. . .] the deity [. . .] lifted up [her eyes . . .] and she [. . . ed, and] she saw [. . .] coming toward her three DANNAs away. [The goddess Kubaba(?)] began to say [to LAMMA:] "First [I have seen] the great gods, the elders, your forefathers. Go to meet them and bow to them." LAMMA began to reply to the goddess Kubaba: "The Primeval Gods are great. They have arisen. (But) [I do not fear] them at all. [Do I] not [put] bread into their mouths? The paths which the w[inds] are to go and come on, those I, LAMMA, king of heaven, allot to the gods." The tempestuous(?) winds brought [LAMMA's evil words] to Ea (while he was) on his way.[7] His [mind became angry]. Ea began to speak to Kumarbi: "Come, let us go back. This LAMMA whom we made king in heaven, just as he himself is complacent(?), so he has made the countries complacent(?), and no one any longer gives bread or drink offerings to the gods."

§7 (A iii 19–30) Ea and Kumarbi turned [their faces]: Ea [went] to Apzuwa, but Kumarbi went away to Tuttul. Ea made a messenger stand up in front [of himself] and undertook to dispatch him to LAMMA (saying): "Go, speak these words to [LAMMA]: 'Ever since we made you king in heaven, [you] have not done anything. You have never convoked [an assembly . . .']." [*The end of the speech is fragmentary.*] The messenger departed and recounted [Ea's words to LAMMA] just so.

§8 (A iii 31–38) When [LAMMA] had heard [Ea's words], he began to [rejoice] within himself. Ea began to say to Izzummi, [his vizier]: "Go down to the Dark Earth, and tell the words which I am speaking to you to

Nara-Napsara, my brother, (saying): 'Take my speech and hearken to my words. [LAMMA] has made me angry, so I have deposed him from the kingship in heaven.'"

§9 (A iii 39–46) "'That LAMMA whom we made king in heaven, just as he himself is complacent(?), so he has made the countries complacent(?), and no one any longer gives bread or drink offerings to the gods. Now, Nara, my brother, hear me. Mobilize all the animals of the earth. Mt. Nasalma [. . .], and unto his head [. . . '"].

[*Gap of undetermined length.*]

§10 (A iv 8–16) [. . .] began to [speak to . . .] before [. . .] who placed the burden [in . . .]. [. . .] began to speak [. . .]. Hear my words. [Hold your ear] inclined [to . . .]. [. . .] wagon [. . .]. His *ikdu* (a body part) from his back [. . .] under 700 [. . .].

§11 (A iv 17–22) [As] Tessub (and) NINURTA, his vizier, [. . . ed], they made LAMMA the same way. They spread/trampled(?) [. . .], [they . . . ed] LAMMA [. . .]. They cut up(?) [. . .] from his back. They cut up [. . .] his *ikdu.*

§12 (A iv 23–30) LAMMA [spoke] back to Tessub: "Tessub, my lord! Long ago [. . .]. To me [. . .]!" Tessub spoke (back) to LAMMA: "Let them proceed to [. . .] (to/from) you. [Let them . . .] (to) me. [Let them . . .] the cup from you quickly(?). I [. . .] it to you."

[*Tablet ends here. Only one sign of the colophon remains.*]

16. The Song of Silver

This myth belongs to the Kumarbi Cycle (Hoffner 1988b). The opening of the text (§§ 1–2) is crucial for this determination. It is said there that Silver is greater in many respects than the well-known deities of the pantheon. Although he might therefore be deserving of a cult of his own, he has none. The singer identifies one of his sources of information about Silver and his background as "wise men" (§2). "Wise men" are also mentioned in the Kumarbi fragment KBo 26.88 i 5. That fragment is not translated in this volume, because its contents are insufficient to prove that it belongs to the Song of Silver. The numbered sections of this myth follow the edition of Hoffner (1988b). Although no part of the Song of Silver is preserved that describes his defeat and dethronement, we may assume this on the basis of the pattern established for other songs in the Kumarbi Cycle.

1. Introduction

§1.1 [Among Tessub], the Sun God of the Sky, Sauska(?), Nineveh's(?) [Queen, and all the gods], no one worships(?) [him], (although) [his] *mal* [is greater than their *mal*s]. His word [is greater(?)] than [their(?)] words, his wisdom [is greater(?)] than [their(?)] wisdom, his battle [and his] glo[ry(?) are greater(?) than theirs, and their(?)] *handatars* [are not(?) greater(?)] for him than his *handatars*.

§1.2 It is Silver the Fine [. . .] whom I sing. Wise men [told(?)] me [the . . . of] the fatherless [boy(?)]. It did not exist. Long ago Silver's [. . . had disappeared(?)]. And his . . . they do not know. [Heroic(?)] men ran to battle. [Abundance(?)] did not exist. And grain [did not grow(?)]. [. . .] hungry(?) [. . .].

2. The Birth of Silver?

Fragment 2 reports a birth. And since Silver is the principal character of this story, as well as the son of Kumarbi, it seems probable that it is his birth which is described.

§2.1 . . . went.

§2.2 [. . .] fire [. . .] of alabaster [. . .] his eyes [. . .] they gave it [. . . . The first, second, third, and] fourth months passed; the fifth(?), [sixth, seventh, eighth, and ninth months passed; and the tenth month] arrives.

§2.3 . . . [His/her tears] flow [like streams]. . . .

3. Silver and the Orphan Boy

Silver is described in this text as a *wannumiyas* DUMU, which means a child whose father is dead or missing. Hittitologists generally translate this as "orphan," but since Silver's mother is still with him, he is not an orphan in the usual sense. There is just a hint that his fatherless condition could be regarded as shameful. This hint is not strong enough to justify a translation "bastard." Silver's consternation at being told by the orphan boy that he too was an orphan need not mean that he was discovering this for the first time. It is unlikely that another child in the community would have more information about this than he. Rather he finds it humiliating to be reminded in public by others that he too was abandoned by his father. This leads him to inquire further about his father from his mother, which he does in fragment 4.

§3.1 In/with power(?). . . .

§3.2 Silver [struck] an orphan boy [with] a stick. The orphan boy spoke an evil word against Silver: "My Silver, why [are you hitting us]? Why are you striking us? You are an orphan like us." [Now when Silver heard these words], he began to weep. Weeping, Silver went into his house. Silver began to repeat the words to his mother: "The boys I struck down in front of the gate are defying me."

§3.3 "I struck a boy with a stick, and he spoke an [evil] word back to me. Hear, O my mother, the words which the orphan boy said to me: 'Why are you hitting [us? Why are you striking] us? [You are an orphan like us.]'"

4. Silver's Quest for Kumarbi

[*First three lines too fragmentary to translate.*]

§4.1 [His mother(?)] took the stick away from [him. . . . His mother] turned around [and] began to reply [to Silver, her son]: "Do [not hit me], O Silver! Do not strike me! The city(?) [you inquire about] I will tell/describe it to you.[8] [Your father(?) is Kumarbi], the Father of the city Urkis.[9] [He . . . s], and he resides in Urkis. [. . .] the lawsuits of all the lands he [satisfactorily] resolves(?). Your brother is Tessub. He is king in heaven. And he is king in the land. Your sister is Sauska, and she is queen in Nineveh. You must [not] fear any [of them]; only one deity [must you fear. He (i.e., Kumarbi) stirs up(?)] the enemy land(s), and the wild animals. From top to bottom [he . . . s]. From bottom to top [he . . . s." Silver] listened to his mother's words. He set out for Urkis. He arrived in Urkis, but he did not find [Kumarbi] in his house. He (Kumarbi) had gone to roam the land(s). He wanders about up(?) in the mountains. [*Text of col. ii breaks off.*]

5. Tasmisu and Tessub

It is presupposed in this fragment that Silver has become king of the gods. Tessub's brother Tasmisu, who is also his vizier, seems to taunt him for his timidity and cowardice.

§5.1 . . . [Tasmisu began] to speak to Tessub: "[Is it] not [possible(?)] for you to thunder? Do you [not] know [how to . . .] ? On(?) the . . . [Silver(?)] has become king, and [now] he [drives(?)] all the deities with a goad(?) of pistachio wood."

§5.2 Tessub [began to] speak (back?) to his vizier: "Come, let us go and eat [. . .]. Our father, [Kumarbi(?)], did not defeat [Silver(?). Will we] now [defeat] Silver?"

§5.3 They took each other by the hand, [the two brothers, and to . . .] they set out. In one stage they made [the trip]. At the city [of . . .] they arrived. They [. . . ed]. On the . . . Silver is sitting like a [shaft(?). They/he] fear[ed(?) him, the . . .], the violent [god . . .].

§5.4 Tessub [and Tasmisu arrived in . . .]. He saw him and [. . .]. [*The text of col. iii breaks off here.*]

6. About Old Men

§6.1 [. . .] the old [men . . .] . . . began to [. . .]. The tree which we will cut for ourselves, you . . . will . . . it up too. What ox you [. . .] in the midst of the vegetable garden, you, O . . . [will . . .] was of the heart. [. . .] by means of whose meadow [. . .] the owner of the meadow [. . .] and they [. . .] the old men [. . .].

7. Silver Threatens the Sun and Moon

This episode could be placed either before or after Silver became king of the gods, although the words "what [lands] you [govern]" are more appropriate to the latter period. It serves to show his great power.

§7.1 [. . .] sent: "Go down [to the Dark Earth and . . .] him [with] a goad(?)" [. . .] began to [. . .].

§7.2 [. . .] he closed up his [. . .] with [. . .] judged [. . .]. And all the gods [. . .] they come/see(?). Silver [seized(?)] power with his hands. Silver seized the spear. He dragged the Sun and Moon down from heaven. The Sun and the Moon did reverence. They bowed to Silver. The Sun and the Moon began to speak to Silver:

§7.3 "[O Silver, our lord], do not strike/kill us! We are the luminaries [of heaven] and [earth]. We are the torches of what [lands] you [govern. If you strike/kill us], you will proceed to govern the dark lands personally." [His] soul within [him was filled with] love. [He had] pity on [. . .].

===== 17. The Song of Hedammu =====

All that we possess of this myth are fragments, the ordering of which is that of the latest edition by Siegelová (1971). Because the translation is based upon an eclectic text, we dispense with the column and line count.

Fragment 1

§1.1 . . . [The Sea God(?)] heard, and his mind within rejoiced(?). He [propped(?)] his foot on a stool. They put a rhyton in the Sea God's hand. The great Sea God began to reply to Kumarbi: "Our matter is settled, Kumarbi, Father of the Gods. Come to my house in seven days, and [I will give you] Sertapsuruhi, my daughter, whose length is [. . .] and whose width is one mile. [You will drink(?)] Sertapsuruhi like sweet cream." When Kumarbi heard (this), his [mind] within him rejoiced. Night fell. [. . .] They brought the great Sea God out of Kumarbi's house accompanied by (the music of) bronze *arkammi-* and *galgalturi-*instruments and escorted him to his house. (There) he sat down on a good chair made of [. . .]. The Sea God waited seven days for Kumarbi.

§1.2 Kumarbi [began] to speak [words] to his vizier: "Mukisanu, my vizier! [Listen carefully to] the words which I speak to you! [. . .]" [. . .]

Fragment 2

This fragment describes the serpent Hedammu's voracious appetite for a wide variety of creatures.[10]

Fragment 5

§5.1 " . . . Sauska, [Queen of Nineveh], comes. [Let them set up a chair for her to sit in]. Let them spread a table for her to eat at." [While they were thus speaking], Sauska reached them. They set up a chair for her [to sit in], but she didn't sit down in it. They decked [a table for her to eat at], but she didn't reach out to it. [They gave her a cup], but [the Queen of Nineveh] didn't put her lip to it. [. . .] began to speak: "Why do you not eat or drink, my lady? [Is it because you don't know it, namely,] food? Is it because you don't know drinking? They [incited(?)] the Sea God against the gods. He [. . .]ed in sky and earth. And what surrogate/usurper shall I [. . .] describe in the Sea?" He described Hedammu [. . .] and Sauska [. . . ed] him.

§5.2 [. . .] heard Sauska, [and became sad. His . . .] . . . s. His [tears flow] forth [like] streams. [. . .]

Fragment 6

§6.1 [Ea], King of Wisdom, spoke among the gods. [The god Ea] began to say: "Why are you [plural] destroying [mankind]? They will not give sacrifices to the gods. They will not burn cedar as incense to you. If you [plural] destroy mankind, they will no longer [worship] the gods. No one will offer [bread] or libations to you [plural] any longer. Even Tessub, Kummiya's heroic king, will himself grasp the plow. Even Sauska and Hebat will themselves grind at the millstones."

§6.2 [Ea], King of Wisdom, said to Kumarbi: "Why are you, O Kumarbi, seeking to harm mankind? Does [not] the mortal take a grain heap and do they not promptly offer (it) to you, Kumarbi? Does he make offering to you alone, Kumarbi, Father of the Gods, joyfully in the midst of the temple? Do they not (also) offer to Tessub, the Canal Inspector of Mankind? And don't they call me, Ea, by name as King? [. . .] you (Kumarbi) are putting wisdom behind [the . . .] of all [. . .]. [. . .] the blood and tears of mankind [. . .] Kumarbi [. . .]." [Breaks off.]

Fragment 7

§7.1 Kumarbi [began to speak] words to [his own mind:] "[Why] would [you] boil(?) [at] me, Kumarbi, like a [. . .], in the place of assembly? [11] Why would you strike me, Ea, [. . .], King of Wisdom? [Why] would you [. . . ?] Why would [you defend(?)] mankind, [. . .] and Ea, foremost [among the gods]?"

§7.2 Kumarbi [spoke] (words) before his mind: "[. . .] me, Kumarbi, son of Alalu(?). But [. . .] me to the god Ammezzadu." In the midst of the gods Kumarbi [raised up Hedammu(?)] like a [. . .] as a surrogate against Tessub. The heroic [. . .] to Tessub [. . . . . .] [Breaks off.]

Fragment 9¹²

§9.1 [. . . " . . . Make your journey] under [river] (and) earth! [Don't let the Moon God], the Sun God or the [gods] of the Dark Earth [see you!] Come up to Kumarbi from beneath [river and] earth!"

§9.2 [Mukisanu] heard the words and [promptly] arose. He made his journey under river and earth. [Neither] the Moon God, the Sun God or the gods of the Dark Earth saw him. He went down to the Sea God.

§9.3 Mukisanu spoke Kumarbi's words to the Sea God: "Come! The Father of the Gods, Kumarbi, is calling you. The matter for which he calls you is urgent. So come promptly! Come away below river and earth! Don't let the Moon God, the Sun God, or the gods of the Dark Earth see you!" When the great Sea God heard the words, he promptly arose and made his journey under river and earth. He traversed (the distance) in one (stage) and came up below Kumarbi's chair from/by . . . and earth. They set up a chair for the Sea God to sit in, and the great [Sea God] sat down in his chair. They placed a table for him set with food. The cupbearer gave him sweet wine to drink. Kumarbi, Father of the Gods, and the great Sea God sat eating and drinking.

§9.4 Kumarbi spoke words to his vizier: "Mukisanu, my vizier! Listen carefully to the words I speak to you! Bolt the door! [. . .] Throw the latch(?). [Let not the . . .] like an aroma(?) (or: like a drop(?)) [. . .]. 'Poor men' [will . . . us(?)] like a. . . . "

§9.5 Mukisanu [heard] the words, and quickly [arose]. He began to [throw] the latch(?) and the [. . .]. And [. . .] bronze [. . .].

Fragment 10

[. . .] a blow [. . .]. The lightning flashes and the [. . .]s of Tessub and Sauska have not yet gone away with the water (i.e., rain?). We have not yet come [. . .]. Our knees tremble [beneath] us. Our head spins like a potter's wheel. Our little family(?)¹³ [. . . s] like. . . .

Fragment 11

§11.1 (Tessub speaks to Sauska:) [. . .] we (i.e., Hedammu and I) will engage in [conflict(?). And . . .] Hedammu [*accusative*]. [. . .] If [I . . .] Hedammu, [it will . . .]. But if Hedammu [. . . s], then it is my fault.

§11.2 [Now when Tessub(?)] finished speaking, [he went] away. [But Sauska] went to the bath house. [The Queen of Nineveh] went there to wash herself. She washed herself. She [. . .]ed. She anointed herself with fine perfumed oil. She adorned herself. And (qualities which arouse) love ran after her like puppies.

§11.3¹⁴ [Sauska] began to say [to Ninatta and] Kulitta: "Take [an *arkammi*-instrument], take a *galgalturi*-instrument. At the sea on the right play the

arkammi, on the left play the *galgalturi.* [. . .] to kingship [. . .]. Perhaps [Hedammu(?)] will hear our message (i.e., song). [. . .] let us see how [. . .]."
   §11.4 [. . .] Ninatta and Kulitta [. . .].

Fragment 12

§12.1 [. . .] Sauska [. . .] Hedammu [. . .] in the deep waters [. . .].
   §12.2 When Hedammu [. . .]s, [. . .]. And Hedammu [. . .]. [He raised(?)] his head from the watery deep. He spied Sauska. Sauska held up her naked members before Hedammu.
   §12.3 Hedammu began to speak words to Sauska: "What deity are you, that [you] do not [. . . ?] You [. . .], and in/to the sea [. . .] . . . " And [Sauska . . . ed] to him as to a bull. [. . .] doesn't know [. . .].

Fragment 13

§13.1 [. . . to] Hedammu [in(?)] the sea [. . .] Sertapsuruhi [. . .].
   §13.2 [. . . to(?)] Hedammu [. . .] began to [say: " . . . . . .] heroic [. . .] he fills [. . .] my mother [. . .] you [*nominative*] [. . .]."

Fragment 14

Hedammu [began] to say to Sauska: "You [. . .] unlike a(ny other) woman. So I will eat you up. [The . . . s] are angry, and they [. . .] to me. [. . .]."

Fragment 15

§15.1 Hedammu spoke words to Sauska: "What kind of woman are you?" Sauska replied to Hedammu: "I am an angry(?) girl. The mountains [spread out(?)] their greenery for me like a woven cloth(?)." Sauska speaks flattery(?) [. . .] to Hedammu, praises(?) him with words and intoxicates him.
   §15.2 Hedammu said to Sauska: "What kind of woman are you, that [. . .] a name [. . .]? I am [. . .]." [*Only bits of the rest of Hedammu's speech are preserved.*]

Fragment 16

§16.1 [. . .] in the sky clouds [. . .] with/from [. . .] waters [. . .] he/she made. When [Sauska], Queen of Nineveh, had approved [the . . .], she filled a love potion(?) — *sahis-* and *parnullis-*wood in "strong" waters and smelled(?) the love potion, the *sahis-* and *parnullis-*wood, in the waters. Now when Hedammu had tasted the aroma, namely, the beer, [sweet] sleep overcame the mind of the valiant Hedammu. He was dozing like an ox (or) ass.[15] He recognizes no [. . .] he keeps on eating frogs and snails(?).

§16.2 [Sauska] said to Hedammu: "Come up again. [Come(?)] from the strong waters. Come through the midst of [. . .]." [Hedammu . . . s] 90,000 [. . .]. He levels(?) a [. . .] place from the earth. Sauska holds out [her naked members toward Hedammu]. Hedammu [sees(?) the beautiful goddess], and his penis springs forth. His penis impregnates [. . .]s. He [. . .]ed 130 cities [. . .]. [He . . . ed] 70 cities with his belly. [. . .] came to an end. [. . .] heaped up piles of heads.

§16.3 Sauska, Queen of Nineveh, was struck [. . .] on/at the. . . . At the second [. . .] she came down [to] Hedammu, and Sauska, [Queen] of Nineveh, walked before him. Sauska came [down to him], and after her Hedammu, like a . . . , pours out [. . .]. They [. . .] it on the earth [like(?)] frightful floods. The valiant Hedammu came down from his throne, from the sea. He came out onto the dry land [. . .].

================ 18. The Song of Ullikummi ================

The final clause of §19 summarizes the overarching theme of the Kumarbi Cycle: Kumarbi, who ironically is "host/parent" for Anu's seed, which becomes Tessub, attempts in each succeeding song of the cycle to raise up someone (Ullikummi, Hedammu, Silver, and LAMMA) to supplant Tessub as king of the gods.

Tablet 1

§1 [*The first part of the opening paragraph is broken away in all the copies of the story.*] (A i 1–4) [. . .] in what mind? [. . . who] takes [wisdom]? It is Kumarbi, Father of All Gods, of whom I sing.[16]

§2 (A i 5–8) Kumarbi takes wisdom into his mind. He raises an "Evil Day" as an evil man. He seeks evil against Tessub. He raises a supplanter against Tessub.

§3 (A i 9–10) Kumarbi [takes] wisdom before his mind and aligns it like a bead (on a string).

§4 (A i 11–16) When Kumarbi [had taken] wisdom [before his mind], he promptly arose from his chair. In his hand he took a staff; [on his feet] he put the swift winds [as shoes]. He set out from the city Urkis and arrived at the Cold Spring.

§5 (B i 13–20) Now in the Cold Spring there lies a great rock: its length is three miles and its breadth is [. . .] and a half miles. His mind leaped forward upon what it has below [17] [. . .], and he slept with the rock. His penis [thrust(?)] into her. He "took" her five times; [again] he "took" her ten times. [*About thirty to thirty-five lives lost.*]

§6 (A ii 1–8) [On the . . .] Kumarbi, Father of the Gods, is sitting. [. . .] saw Kumarbi and set out for the sea [. . .].

§7 (A ii 9–13) Impaluri began to speak words to the Sea God: "What [has(?)] my lord [. . . ed] me? [. . .] to the side of the sea. I saw [. . .] Kumarbi, the Father of the Gods, is sitting [. . .]."

§8 (A ii 14–19, C ii 7–21) [When the Sea God] heard the words of Impaluri, the Sea God replied to Impaluri: "Impaluri, [my vizier]! [Hold] your ear [cocked] to the words which I shall speak to you. [Go] speak these weighty [words before Kumarbi]. Go speak to Kumarbi: 'Why have you come against my house in anger? Trembling has seized the house. Fear has seized the servants. In anticipation of you cedar has already been broken. In anticipation of you food has already been cooked. In anticipation of you the musicians hold their *ISHTAR*-instruments in readiness day and night. Arise and come back home to my house.'" So Kumarbi arose, and Impaluri went before him. But Kumarbi [. . .]. So Kumarbi set out and went into the Sea God's house.

§9 (C ii 22–37) And the Sea God said: "Let them set for Kumarbi a stool to sit on. Let them set a table before him. Let them bring him food and drink. Let them bring beer for him to drink." The cooks brought cooked dishes. The cupbearers brought him sweet wine to drink. They drank once, twice, three times, four times, five times, six times, seven times, and Kumarbi [began] to say to Mukisanu, his vizier: "Mukisanu, my vizier! Hold [out] your ear to the word which I shall speak to you. In your hand take a staff; [on your feet] put on shoes, and go [. . .]. In the waters [. . . . Speak(?) these] words before the waters. [. . .] Kumarbi [. . . "]. [*Break of about twenty lines.*]

§10 (A iii 1–9) [. . .] when from the dark [. . .] the watch arrived [. . .]. And (s)he [. . . ed] the stone. [They(?)] made her give birth [. . .]. The rock [. . .] the son of Kumarbi [was] glorious(?).

§11 (A iii 10–14) [The . . .] women made her give birth. The Fate Goddesses and the Mother Goddesses [lifted the child] and cradled [him] on Kumarbi's knees. Kumarbi began [to amuse] that boy, and he began to clean(?) him, and he gave [to the child(?)] a fitting name.

§12 (A iii 15–25) Kumarbi began to say to himself: "What name [shall I put on] the child whom the Fate Goddesses and Mother Goddesses have given to me? He sprang forth from the body like a shaft. Henceforth let Ullikummi be his name. Let him go up to heaven to kingship. Let him sup-press the fine city of Kummiya. Let him strike Tessub. Let him chop him up fine like chaff. Let him grind him under foot [like] an ant. Let him snap off Tasmisu like a brittle reed. Let him scatter all the gods down from the sky like flour. Let him smash them [like] empty pottery bowls."

§13 (A iii 26–36) When Kumarbi had finished saying these words, he said to himself: "To whom shall I give this child? Who will [take] him and treat him like a gift? [Who . . . ? Who will carry the child] to the Dark Earth? The Sun God of [the Sky and the Moon God] must not see him. Tessub, the heroic King of Kummiya, must not [see him] and kill him. Sauska, the Queen of Nineveh, the one of the . . . woman, must not see him and snap him off like a brittle reed."

§14 (A iii 37–45) Kumarbi began to say to Impaluri: "Impaluri, hold your ear cocked to the words which I shall speak to you. In your hand take a staff; on your feet put shoes like the swift winds. Go to the Irsirra deities and speak before the Irsirra deities these important words: 'Come! Kumarbi, Father of the Gods, is calling you to the house of the gods. The matter about which he calls you [. . .]. So come quickly.'"

§15 (A iii 46–48, C iii 4–8) "'The [Irsirra deities] will take the child and [carry] it to the [Dark] Earth. The Irsirra deities [. . .], the . . . s. But he [will] not [. . .] to the great [. . .]s.'" And [when] Impaluri [heard these words, he took] a staff in his hand, he put [shoes on his feet]. Impaluri [went forth] and came to the Irsirra deities.

§16 (C iii 9–19) [Impaluri began to speak] words to the Irsirra deities: "Come. Kumarbi, Father of the Gods, [is calling you]. You do not know the matter about which [he is calling] you. So come quickly." So when the Irsirra deities heard the words, [they hastened] and hurried. They [rose from their chairs], made the trip in one stage, and arrived where Kumarbi was. Then Kumarbi began to speak to the Irsirra deities:

§17 (C iii 20–27) "Take this [child] and treat it like a gift. Carry it to the Dark Earth. Hasten, hurry. Place it on Ubelluri's right shoulder. Each day let it grow one *AMMATU* higher. Each month let it grow IKU higher.[18] Whatever stone strikes(?) its head, may it do it no harm(?)."[19]

§18 (A iv 6–12) Now when the Irsirra deities heard these words, they took [the child] from Kumarbi's knees. The Irsirra deities lifted the child and pressed it to their breast like a garment. They lifted it [like] the winds(?) and cradled it on Ellil's knees. Ellil lifted his eyes and saw the child, standing before the god, his body made of basalt stone.

§19 (A iv 13–19) Then Ellil began to say to himself, "What child is this whom the Fate Goddesses and Mother Goddesses have raised again?[20] Who can [any longer] bear the intense struggles of the great gods? This evil (plot) can only be Kumarbi's. Just as Kumarbi raised Tessub, so (now) he has raised against him this Basalt as a supplanter."

§20 (A iv 20–21) When Ellil [finished speaking] these words, [they placed(?)] the child on Ubelluri's right shoulder [like a shaft].

§21 (A iv 22–26) The Basalt kept growing. The strong [. . .]s kept raising it. Each day it grew one *AMMATU* higher; each month it grew one IKU higher. Whatever stone struck(?) its head did it no harm(?).[21]

§22 (A iv 27–32) When the fifteenth day arrived (and the Basalt had grown to a height of half an IKU), the Stone was high: it was standing like a shaft with the sea coming up to its knees. The Stone came out of the water. In height it was like a [. . .]. The sea reached to the place of its [. . .] belt like a garment. The Basalt was lifted up like a . . . . In the sky above it meets temples and a *kuntarra*-shrine.

§23 (A iv 33–36) The Sun God looked [down] from the sky and saw Ullikummi. Ullikummi saw the Sun God of the Sky. The Sun God began to say to himself, "What quickly growing deity [stands] there in the sea? His body is unlike that of all the other gods."

§24 (A iv 37–40) The Sun God of the Sky turned his rays and proceeded to the sea. When the Sun God reached the sea, he held his hand to his forehead. [He got a] close [look] at Ullikummi. From anger his appearance changed.

§25 (A iv 41–48) When the Sun God of the Sky saw the god E[llil], he turned his rays around again and proceeded to where Tessub was. [Tasmisu] saw the Sun God coming and said to Tessub, "Why is the Sun God of the Sky, [King] of the Lands, coming? On what business does he come? The matter must be [important]. It must be something [not] to be disregarded. The struggle must be severe. The battle must be severe. It must entail uproar in heaven and famine and death in the land."

§26 (A iv 49–50) Tessub said to Tasmisu, "Let them set up a chair for him to sit in; let them lay a table for him to eat from."

§27 (A iv 51–54) And while they were speaking thus, the Sun God approached them. A chair was set up for him to sit in, but he wouldn't sit down. A table was laid for him to eat from, but he wouldn't touch a thing. A cup was offered to him, but he wouldn't put his lip to it.

§28 (A iv 55–58) Tessub began to say to the Sun God, "Is it because the chamberlain set up the chair so badly, that you will not sit down? Is it because (my) table man who set the table is so bad, that you will not eat? Is it because the cupbearer offered you [the cup] so badly, that you will not drink?"

§29 (Colophon:) "Tablet one of the Song of Ullikummi [. . .]."

Tablet 2

§30 [*The beginning is broken. Apparently after explaining why he will not observe the amenities of hospitality until he has delivered his urgent message, the Sun God tells Tessub the bad news about Ullikummi.*]

§31 (B i 1–13) [When] Tessub heard [these words], his appearance changed because of his anger. But [to the Sun God of the Sky] Tessub said, "Let [the food on the table] become appetizing [to you] and eat [your fill]. Let [the wine in the cup] become appetizing [to you] and drink your fill. [Then get up] and go up to the sky." The Sun God of the Sky rejoiced when he heard [these words], he rejoiced. [The food on the table] became appetizing [to him], so that he ate. [The wine in his cup] became appetizing [to him], so that he drank. [The Sun God] got up and went up to the sky.

§32 (B i 14–28) After (the departure) of the Sun God of the Sky Tessub formed a plan in his mind. Tessub and Tasmisu joined hands and went out of the *kuntarra*-shrine and the temple. Sauska too came from the sky looking formidable. Sauska said to herself, "Where are my two brothers running to?" Boldly(?) Sauska approached. She came up to her brothers. Then they all joined hands and went up Mount Hazzi. (Tessub), the King of Kummiya, set his eye. He set his eye upon the dreadful Basalt. He beheld the dreadful Basalt, and because of anger his appearance changed.

§33 (B i 29–41) Tessub sat down on the ground, and his tears flowed like streams. Tearfully Tessub said, "Who can [any longer] behold the struggle of such a one? Who go on fighting? Who can behold the terrors of such a one any longer?" Sauska said to Tessub, "My brother, he doesn't know/recognize even a little *mal,* but warlikeness has been given to him tenfold. And you do not know the *mal* of the child whom [the . . . s] will bear to them. [. . .] we are in the house of Ea. If I were a [. . .] man, you would be [. . .]. But I will go [and . . .]." [*Text breaks away here until the end of the column.*]

§34 (B ii 1–4) [*Preserves only beginning of the lines.*] "They who [. . .], as the watery d[eep(?) . . . , so] let the [. . . s] be [. . . ed].

§35 (B ii 5–12) [Sauska(?)] dressed and ornamented herself [with . . .]. From Nineveh she [came to the sea(?). She took(?)] the BALAG.DI and the *galgalturi*-instruments in her hand. Sauska set out. She fumigated with cedar. She struck the BALAG.DI and the *galgalturi.* She set the "gold things" in motion, and she took up a song, and heaven and earth echoed it back.

§36 (B ii 13–25) Sauska kept on singing and put on herself a seashell and a pebble (as adornment). A great wave(?) ⟨arose⟩ out of the sea. The great wave(?) said to Sauska, "For whose benefit are your singing? For whose benefit are you filling your mouth with wind? The man (meaning Ullikummi) is deaf; he can[not] hear. He is blind in his eyes; he cannot see. He has no compassion. So go away, Sauska, and find your brother before he (Ullikummi) becomes really valiant, before the skull of his head becomes really terrifying.

§37 (B ii 26–30) When Sauska heard this, she extinguished [the burning cedar]; she laid down [the BALAG.DI and *galgalturi*-instruments], and [she stilled] the "gold things." Tearful she set out [for . . .]. [*Two or three more lines badly damaged.*]

§38 [*Ten lines at the beginning of column iii are very badly damaged. Tessub is addressing Tasmisu:*] (B iii 3–14) "Let them mix fodder. Let them [bring] fine oil and anoint the horns of the bull named Serisu. Let them plate with gold the tail of the bull named Tella. Let them turn the axle(?). On the inside let them move their strong things. On the outside let them release strong stones for the . . . . Let them call forth the stormy weather. Let them summon the rains and winds which break the rocks at ninety IKUs, which cover eight hundred. Let them bring forth from the bedchamber the lightning which flashes terribly. Let them put forward the wagons. Afterward (you) prepare and ready them, and bring me back word.

§39 (B iii 15–24) Now when Tasmisu heard the words, he hurried and hastened. [He drove] the bull Serisu [here] from the pasture. [He drove] the bull Tella [here] from Mount Imgarra. [He tied them up] in the outer gate complex. He brought fine oil and [anointed the horns] of the bull Serisu. He [plated with gold] the tail of the bull Tella. [He turned] the axle(?). [On the inside] he [moved their strong things]. On the outside he released [the strong] stones [for the . . . . He called forth the stormy weather. He summoned the rains and winds] which [break the rocks for a distance of ninety IKUs]. [*The rest of column iii is broken away.*]

§40 [*In the few broken lines which remain of column iv the first battle between Tessub and Ullikummi seems to be described.*] (B iv 1–14) [. . .] at five hundred meters (Tessub) approached for battle. He held a weapon and wagons. He brought forth clouds from the sky. Tessub set his eye upon the Basalt and saw it. In height it was [. . .]. But subsequently it tripled its height.

§41 (B iv 15ff.) Then Tessub said to Tasmisu, "[. . .] wagons [. . .] let them go [. . .] summon [. . .]" and he went [. . .] words [. . .]. [*About twenty lines lost.*]

§42 (Colophon:) Tablet two, incomplete, of the Song [of Ullikummi].

Tablet 3

§43 [*Beginning thirty lines lost.*] (A i 2–24) When the gods heard the word, they prepared the wagons and assigned [. . .]. Astabi sprang [upon his wagon like a . . .] and [. . . ed on] the wagon. [. . .] he arrayed the wagons, [. . .] Astabi thundered [. . .], and with thunder Astabi [. . .] let go down to the sea. They drew [water with a . . .]. And Astabi [. . . ed]. Seventy gods seized [. . .]. But still [. . .] was not able. And Astabi [. . .], and the seventy gods [fell(?)] down into the sea. [. . .] the Basalt, (his) body [. . .] and he shook the sky, he [. . .]ed [. . .]. [. . .] shook out the [sky] like an empty[22] garment. The Basalt grew [. . .] tall. Before him the height was 1,900 and . . . DANNAs. It stands below on the Dark Earth. The Basalt is lifted up like a . . . . It meets the *kuntarra*-shrine and the temples. Its height is (now) 9,000 DANNAs. The Basalt [. . .]. Its width is (also) 9,000 DANNAs. It took its stand before the gates of the city Kummiya (Tessub's city) like a shaft. The Basalt stopped Hebat in the temple, so that Hebat no longer hears the message of the gods, nor does she see Tessub or Suwaliyat with her eyes.

§44 (A i 25–29) Hebat spoke these words to Takiti: "[. . .] I do not hear the important word of Tessub [my] lord. Nor do I hear the message of Suwaliyat and all the gods. Perhaps that Ullikummi, the Basalt, of whom they speak, has overcome my husband, the honored/mighty [. . .].

§45 (A i 30–33) Again Hebat said to Takiti, "Hear my words. Take a staff in hand; put shoes on your feet like the winged winds. Go [to . . .]. Perhaps the Basalt has killed [my husband, Tessub, the] mighty king. [Bring] me [back] word.

§46 (A i 34–37) [When Takiti heard the words], he hastened and hurried. [He . . .] drew forth [. . .] goes. But there is no road [. . .] to Hebat [he came(?)].

§47 (A i 38) [Takiti said to Hebat], "My lady, [. . .]" [*About twenty lines to the bottom of column i lost.*]

§48 (A ii 1–16) When Tasmisu heard Tessub's words, he quickly arose, [took] a staff in hand, put shoes on his feet like the winged winds, and went up on the high watchtowers (of his castle). He took [his place] facing Hebat (and said), "[. . .] me to the Little Place²³ until he fulfills the years which have been decreed for him." Now when Hebat saw Tasmisu, she almost fell down from the roof. Had she taken a step, she would have fallen down from the roof. But her female attendants seized her and didn't let go of her. And when Tasmisu had finished speaking the word, he came down from the watchtowers and went to Tessub. Tasmisu said to Tessub, "Where shall we sit down there upon Mount Kandurna? [If(?)] we sit down on Mount Kandurna, another(?) will be sitting on Mount Lalapaduwa. Where will we transport [. . .]? Up in heaven there will be no king."

§49 (A ii 17–26) [Tasmisu] spoke again to Tessub, "[Hear] my words, my lord Tessub. Incline [your ear] to the words which I speak to you. Come, let us go to Apzuwa, before Ea [. . .]. Let us ask for the tablets containing the ancient words. [When] we come before the gate of the house of Ea, we will bow [five times] at Ea's door and [again] five times at Ea's inner door(?). [When] we come [before] Ea, we will bow fifteen times before Ea. Perhaps [it will become pleasant] to Ea by means of . . . ; perhaps Ea [will listen(?)] and have pity on us and personally show us [the tablets containing] the ancient [words]."

§50 (A ii 27–32) [When Tessub] heard the words [of Tasmisu], he hastened [and hurried]. He quickly arose from his chair. [Tessub and Tasmisu] joined hands and made the trip in one stage, and they [arrived] at Apzuwa. [Tessub] went to the house of Ea. [He bowed five times] at the first [door], he bowed five times at the inner door(?). [When] they arrived before Ea, he bowed [fifteen times before Ea].

[*Seven lines of very fragmentary text follow and then the text is completely lost.*]

§51 (A ii 3–6) [. . .] began to speak [. . .] to me the word [. . .]. You, O Tessub, [. . .] before me. Let [. . .] stand up before [. . .]. And wor[d(s) . . .].

§52 (A ii 7–12) When Tasmisu [heard] the words, he ran forth [from . . .], he [kissed(?)] him on the knees three times; he kissed him on the ankles(?) four times. He fought/struggled [. . .] to him [. . .] while to him [. . .] to the Basalt death on the right [shoulder . . .].

§53 (A ii 13–19) Ea spoke to Tasmisu, "[. . .] on Mount Kandurna [. . .] on Mount Lalapaduwa [. . .] on the Dark Earth [. . . the ancient], fatherly, grandfatherly [tablets, and bring] forth the copper cutting tool, and [cut] off [Ullikummi, the Basalt], under his feet. [. . .]."

§54 (A ii 20–23) [When] Ea [finished speaking] the words, [he . . .] in Mount [Kandurna . . . , . . . in M]ount Lalapaduwa [. . . said] to himself [. . .].

§55 (F i? 1–11) [*In a short and broken fragment Tessub meets Ea, and the latter is angered by his presence.*]

§56 (A iii 1–10) [. . .] joined hands [. . .] while [. . .] came forth from the assembly [. . . Ellil(?)] began to weep [and said], "May you live, Ea! [. . .] who comes back before [. . .] the aroma(?) of the gods [. . .]. Why did you/he(?) cross it? [. . .]"

§57 (A iii 11–18) Ea [said] to Ellil, "[Don't you know, Ellil? Has no one brought] you word? [Do you not know him whom Kumarbi created] as a supplanter against Tessub? [The Basalt which] grew [in the water is 9,000 DANNAs] in height. He is lifted up like a . . . [. . .] against you [. . .] primeval [. . . "].

§58 (A iii 19–22) [*Five more fragmentary lines, which mention the "sacred temples."*]

§59 (A iii 24–29) When Ea [finished speaking] the words, [he went] to Ubelluri. [. . .] Ubelluri [lifted] his eyes [and saw Ea]. Ubelluri [spoke words] to Ea, "May you live long, O Ea!" [Ea stood] up [and spoke] a greeting to Ubelluri: "[May you] live, [Ubelluri, you] on whom the heaven and earth are built!"

§60 (A iii 30–39) Ea spoke to Ubelluri, "Don't you know, Ubelluri? Has no one brought you word? Do you not know the swiftly rising god whom Kumarbi created against the gods, and that Kumarbi is . . . planning death against Tessub, and is creating against him a supplanter? Do you not know the Basalt which grew in the water? It is lifted up like a . . . . It has blocked heaven, the holy temples, and Hebat. Is it because you, Ubelluri, are remote from the Dark Earth, that you are unaware of this swiftly rising god?"

§61 (A iii 40–44) Ubelluri spoke to Ea, "When they built heaven and earth upon me, I was aware of nothing. And when they came and cut heaven and earth apart with a copper cutting tool, I was even unaware of that. But now something makes my right shoulder hurt, and I don't know who this god is."

§62 (A iii 45–47) When Ea heard those words, he went around Ubelluri's right shoulder, and (there) the Basalt stood on Ubelluri's right shoulder like a shaft.

§63 (A iii 48–55) Ea spoke to the Primeval Gods, "Hear my words, O Primeval Gods, who know the primeval words. Open again the old, fatherly, grandfatherly storehouses. Let them bring forth the seal of the primeval fathers and with it reseal them. Let them bring forth the primeval copper cutting tool with which they cut apart heaven and earth. We will cut off Ullikummi, the Basalt, under his feet, him whom Kumarbi raised against the gods as a supplanter (of Tessub)."

§64 [*The first twenty-six lines of column iv are broken away.*] (A iv 4–8) Tasmisu [. . .] bowed down [. . .] began to say [. . .]. In his body the [. . .]s have been changed. On his head the hairs changed their appearance.

§65 (A iv 9–12) Ea spoke to Tasmisu, "Go away from in front of me, my son. Do not stand up in front of me. My mind within me has become sad/angry, for with my eyes I have seen the dead, seeing the dead in the Dark Earth, and they are standing like dusty and . . . ones."

§66 (A iv 13–20) Ea spoke to Tasmisu, "First I routed [. . .] Ullikummi, the Basalt. Now go fight him again. Don't let it stand any longer in the gate(s) of the . . . like a shaft." Tasmisu heard and rejoiced. He clapped three times, and up in the sky the gods heard. He clapped a second time, and Tessub, the valiant King of Kummiya, heard. Then they came to the place of assembly, and all the gods began to bellow like cattle at Ullikummi.

§67 (A iv 21–22) Tessub leaped up into his wagon like a . . . and with thunder came down to the sea. Tessub fought the Basalt.

§68 (A iv 23–24) The Basalt spoke to Tessub, "What can I say to you, Tessub? Keep attacking. Be of his mind, for Ea, King of Wisdom, is on your side."

§69 (A iv 25–28) "What can I say to you, Tessub? I held [counsel(?)], and before my mind I lined up wisdom like (a string of) bead(s) as follows: 'I will go up to heaven to kingship. I will take to myself Kummiya, [the gods'] holy temples, and the kuntarras-shrine. I will scatter the gods down from the sky like flour.'"

§70 (A iv 29–39) Ullikummi spoke again to Tessub, "[Behave] like a man again [. . .]. Ea, the King of Wisdom, stands on your side." [. . .] he takes away. And let them go [. . .] to the mountains. Let them [. . .] in the land the high [. . .]. My liver and lung [. . .] let them go. In the land [. . .] those who [. . .]ed up, [. . .] let them [. . .]" [. . .] said, "Long ago [. . .] me [. . .]. What name [shall I give] to him, [. . .]?" [Rest broken away.]

§71 (An unplaced fragment, III E₂ iii 1–5) [. . .] the Basalt [. . .] he performs [. . .] Tessub, the mother of the god Ea [. . .] joined your side [. . .].

§72 (E₂ iii 6–13) I spoke wisdom to myself [. . .] took wisdom into [. . .] mind [. . .] spoke as follows: [" . . .] let him go up to heaven; [let him take] Kummiya, [the fine city; let him strike Tessub, heroic King] of Kummiya; [let him scatter] the gods [down from the sky like flour.]" [The rest is broken away.]

Notes

1. We do not know how many "songs" originally made up the cycle. It is possible that, in addition to the fragments listed by Laroche (1971) under CTH 346, we should consider CTH 350 (fragments naming ISHTAR/Sauska) as belonging to the cycle. These pieces have not been included in this volume.

2. That Hedammu is male is clear from Sauska's enticing him sexually.

3. Or: "because."

4. The point of the question may be that Ea is not at this time in the camp of Kumarbi and should not be antagonized needlessly, or it may be that Seri considers Ea a particularly dangerous opponent.

5. The meaning is that although the fire underneath burns the bottom of the pot, it will be doused with the boiling hot contents, when the pot boils over. Tauri is merely repeating the curses of Tessub which he has heard. But since those curses are extremely unpleasant to Ea, he warns his messenger that he too may "get burned"!

6. The "king" is the same god who in iv 18–19 from his throne approved of the birth of Earth's two sons. He now gives gifts either to the two sons or to their mother Earth.

7. Variant adds the words "When Ea heard LAMMA's words."

8. From what follows it is clear that what the mother tells Silver is his family, using the city of Urkis as a point of departure.

9. If this myth reflects the genealogy of the Kumarbi Cycle, the real father of the Storm God was Anu. But since Anu's seed was implanted in Kumarbi, there is a sense in which his father was Kumarbi. Apparently, Silver was the son of Kumarbi by a mortal woman and the stepbrother of Tessub, Sauska, and of Tasmisu through the common father Kumarbi.

10. It is possible, but not certain, that the words "They raise up Hedammu against [Tessub(?)]" in lines 5–6 indicate that he, like Ullikummi, is Kumarbi's surrogate. No account of Hedammu's birth is preserved, but it is likely that he is the offspring of Kumarbi's union with Sertapsuruhi.

11. Since Kumarbi's words are addressed to Ea, one is reminded of Ea's words to Tauri at the end of Text 14 (A iii 67–72) about his own anger boiling over like a pot on those who curse him.

12. See Fragment 28, not translated here, for a related text.

13. Or perhaps: "our goat kid."

14. Siegelová's edition needs to be augmented here with KBo 22.51.

15. Perhaps meaning that he slept standing up.

16. Text 16 provides another example of this opening. Its significance is explained in Hoffner (1988b).

17. A reference to the rock's genitals.

18. This suggests a 1:30 ratio between the *AMMATU* and the *IKU*. The absolute value of these units is currently disputed.

19. The meaning is uncertain. The Hittite is literally translated: "Whatever stone is struck upon its head, may it be clothed upon its eye(s)."

20. It is possible that the word "again" alludes to an earlier "song" in the Kumarbi cycle where the Fate Goddesses and the Mother Goddesses raised another offspring of Kumarbi. See the introduction to the Hurrian myths.

21. Thus Kumarbi's prophecy of §17 (C iii 20–27) begins to be fulfilled.

22. Or: "unornamented."

23. That is, he must leave his throne.

III

Tales Involving
Deities and Mortals

---

19. A Tale of Two Cities
Kanesh and Zalpa

This story serves as the introduction to a semihistorical account of political rela-
tions between the early Hittite state and the city of Zalpa on the Black Sea (del Monte
and Tischler 1978: 490–92; Hoffner 1980). The motif of exposing boy babies and
keeping girl babies reminds one of the legend of the Amazons, who according to later
Greek traditions lived in Anatolia.

§1 (A obv. 1–5) [The Queen] of Kanesh once bore thirty sons in a single
year. She said: "What a horde is this which I have born!" She caulked(?)
baskets with dung, put her sons in them, and launched them in the river. The
river carried them down to the sea at the land of Zalpuwa. But the gods took
them up out of the sea and reared them.

§2 (A obv. 6–20) When some years had passed, the queen again gave birth,
this time to thirty daughters. This time she herself reared them. Now the sons
were on their way back to Kanesh, driving a donkey. When they reached the
city of Tamarmara, they said: "Heat up a bedroom, and our donkey will
climb up (a staircase)!" At this the men of the city replied: "What have we
come to, that a donkey can climb up (a staircase)?" The boys countered:
"What have we come to, that a woman can give birth to [thirty] children [in
a single year]? Yet one did give birth to us all in one pregnancy!" (Not to be
outdone,) the men of the city retorted: "Our Queen of Kanesh also gave birth
to thirty daughters in one pregnancy. (Her) sons (born earlier) have
vanished." The boys said to each other: "We have found our mother, whom
we were seeking! Come, let us go to Kanesh!" Now when they had gone to
Kanesh, the gods put another . . . in them, so that their mother didn't

62

recognize them. She wanted to give her daughters in marriage to her sons. The older sons didn't recognize their sisters. But the youngest [objected:] "Should we take our own sisters in marriage? Don't do such an impious thing! [It is surely not] right that [we should] sleep with them." [*The first column of the text, which contained the entire legend, now breaks off.*]

══════════ 20. Appu and His Two Sons ══════════

I have treated this text as an independent story. According to Güterbock (1946) the text is continued in the tale of the Sun God, the Cow, and the Fisherman (Text 21). Although the extant copies of Text 20 are New Hittite, archaic grammatical elements indicate an archetype composed in the Old or Middle Hittite period. The story has a moral, which is stated in the proemium. The unnamed deity who is praised for always vindicating the just person will also thwart the evil son of Appu, who attempts to defraud his honest brother. Only a little bit of the beginning of the composition is lost. Where the text becomes available some sort of a proemium is in progress.

§1 (1 i 1–6) He/she it is (i.e., some deity) who always exonerates just men, but chops down evil men like trees, repeatedly striking evil men on their skulls (like) . . . s until he/she destroys them.

§2 (1 i 7–12) There was a city named Sudul. It was situated on the seacoast in the land of Lulluwa. Up there lived a man named Appu. He was the richest man in all the land. He had many cattle and sheep.

§3 (1 i 13–14) He had accumulated silver, gold, and lapis lazuli like a whole heap of threshed grain.

§4 (1 i 15–21) There was nothing which he lacked but one thing: he had neither son nor daughter. The elders of Sudul sat eating in his presence. One gave bread and a piece of grilled meat to his son; another gave his son a drink. But Appu had no one to whom to give bread.

§5 (1 i 22–26) The table was covered with a linen cloth and stood in front of the altar. Appu arose, went home, and lay on his bed with his shoes on.

§6 (1 i 27–30) Appu's wife questioned their servants: "He has never had success(?) before. You don't think he has now had success(?), do you?" The woman went and lay down with Appu with her clothes on.

§7 (1 i 31–37) Appu awoke from his sleep, and his wife questioned him: "You have never had success(?) before. Have you now been successful(?)?" When Appu heard this, he replied: "You are a woman and think like one. You know nothing at all."

§8 (1 i 38–45) Appu rose from his bed, took a white lamb, and set out to meet the Sun God. The Sun God looked down from the sky, changed himself into a young man, came to him, and questioned him: "What is your problem, that [I may solve] it for you?"

§9 (1 ii 1–9) When [Appu] heard this, he replied to him: "[The gods] have given me wealth. They have given [me cattle and sheep(?)]. I lack only one thing: I have neither son nor daughter." When the Sun God heard this, he said: "Go get drunk, go home, and have good sexual intercourse with your wife. The gods will give you one son."

§10 (1 ii 10–18) When Appu heard this, he went back home, but the Sun God went back up to the sky. Now Tessub saw the Sun God coming three DANNAs distant, and said to his vizier: "Look who's coming: the Sun God, Shepherd of the Lands! You don't suppose that somewhere the land is laid waste? Might not cities somewhere be devastated? Might not troops somewhere be put to rout?

§11 (1 ii 19–24) Instruct the cook and cupbearer to provide him with food and drink." [The Sun God] came, [. . .], and [Tessub . . . ed] him there. Tessub [. . . ed] the Sun God, and began to question him:

§12 (1 ii 25–30) "Why [have you come, O Sun God of the Sky? . . . "] [*Long break.*]

§13 (1 iii 1–6) [*Beginning of column iii broken.*]

§14 (1 iii 7–16) Appu's wife became pregnant. The first month, the second month, the third month, the fourth month, the fifth month, the sixth month, the seventh month, the eighth month, the ninth month passed, and the tenth month arrived. Appu's wife bore a son. The nurse lifted the boy and placed him on Appu's knees. Appu began to amuse the boy and to clean(?) him off. He put a fitting name upon him: "Since my paternal gods didn't [take] the right way for him, but kept to a wrong way, let his name be Wrong."

§15 (1 iii 17–20) Again, a second time Appu's wife became pregnant. The [tenth] month arrived, and the woman bore a son. The nurse lifted [the boy] and (Appu) put the right name upon him, "Let them call him the right name."

§16 (1 iii 21–22) "Since my paternal gods took the right way for him, let his name be Right."

§17 (1 iii 23–24) [Appu's boys] grew up and matured and came into manhood.

§18 (1 iv 1–3) [When] Appu's boys had grown up [and matured] and come into manhood, they parted [from] Appu, and [divided up] the estate.

§19 (1 iv 4–12) Brother Wrong said to Brother Right: "Let us part and settle down in different places." Brother Right said [to Brother Wrong]: "Then who [. . .]?" Brother Wrong said to Brother Right: "Since the mountains dwell separately, since the rivers flow in separate courses, as the very gods dwell separately—I say these things to you:

§20 (1 iv 13–20) "The Sun God dwells in Sippar. The Moon God dwells in Kuzina. Tessub dwells in Kummiya. And Sauska dwells in Nineveh. Nanaya [dwells] in Kissina. And Marduk dwells in Babylon. As the gods dwell separately, so let us settle in different places."

§21 (1 iv 21–25) Wrong and Right began to divide up (the estate), while the Sun God looked down from heaven. Brother Wrong took [a half] and gave the other half to his brother Right.

§22 (1 iv 26–33) They [. . .]ed among themselves. There was one plow ox and [one] cow. Wrong took the one good plow ox, and [gave] the bad cow to his brother Right. The Sun God looked [down] from heaven (and said): "Let [Right's bad] cow become good, and let her bear [. . .]."

§23 (1 iv 34) (Colophon:) First tablet of Appu: incomplete.

[*A separate fragment, numbered 16 by Siegelová, offers part of the continuation. Beginning broken away.*]

§24 (16:4–5) [But when they] arrived in Sippar and took their stand before the Sun God for judgment, [the Sun God] awarded the judgment to Brother Right.

§25 (16:6–9) [Then Brother Wrong] began to curse. The Sun God heard the curses [and] said: "I will not [decide] it for you. Let Sauska, Nineveh's Queen, decide it for you."

§26 (16:10–12) [Wrong and Right] set out. And when they arrived at Nineveh and stood before Sauska [for judgment, . . .] drew one IKU in one direction [and . . . in the other direction]. [*Rest of the text lost.*]

═══════ **21. The Sun God, the Cow, and the Fisherman** ═══════

§1 (ii 46–59) [. . .] the olive tree [. . .] prominent [. . .] they used to drive [. . .] he left [. . .] *artarti*-tree [. . .] tender plant growth(?). He [. . .]ed his soul. The cow thrived and . . . ed. The Sun God looked down from the sky, and his desire leaped forward upon the cow. [He became] a young man, came down from the sky, and began to speak to the cow: "Who do you think you are, that you continually graze on our meadow [. . .]? When the grass is tender and young, [and you graze here], you destroy the meadow."

§2 (ii 60–64) [The cow] replied: "Is [. . .] hire [. . .] in its [. . .]?" Then the Sun God responded: "[. . .] and it [is] in bloom [. . .] me [. . .]." [The Sun God] spoke [further] to the cow: "[. . .]" [*The rest of the column is broken away, as are the first four lines of the next column.*]

§3 (iii 5) [. . .] to you [. . .].

§4 (iii 6–7) The Sun God [replied] to the cow: "[What . . .] knows, [. . .] to me."

§5 (iii 8–14) The Sun God drove the cow [. . .], and the Sun God [. . .] the cow, [and . . .] cattle [. . .][1]

§6 (iii 15–27) The cow [. . .]. [*Most of three lines missing.*] the second, third, [fourth, fifth, sixth, seventh, eighth], ninth, and tenth month arrived, [and the cow gave birth]. The cow [called] back up to the sky [and] glowered [at the Sun God]. She said [to the Sun God]: "Now I ask you please: [My calf] should have four legs. Why have I borne this two-legged thing?" Like a lion, the cow opened her mouth and went toward the child to eat (it?). The cow made her . . . as deep as the Deep Blue and set out toward the child [to . . .].

§7 (iii 28–31) The Sun God looked down from the sky. [He came down(?)] and took his stand beside the cow. He began [to say to her:] "And who are you, [that you have approached . . .] to gulp down [. . .]?"

§8 (iii 32–33) The Sun God [. . . ed] the cow [and . . .]. And (s)he [. . . ed] to [. . .].

§9 (iii 34–36) When the child [. . . ed, . . .] grass [. . .] his eyes [. . .].

§10 (iii 37–38) The Sun God [. . .] and him [. . .]

[*Break of about 17 lines.*]

§11 (iii 56–60) "The great rivers [. . .] are troubled. The [. . .] are troubled for washing. [. . .] of blood [. . .] for washing. [. . .] let it/him keep on living." The day becomes warm [. . .].

§12 (iii 61–70) When the Sun God had set out to go back up to the sky, he [. . . ed] the child [. . .]. He strokes(?) its members along with [its head]. The Sun God spoke to Sa[. . .]: "Take a staff in hand, put the winds on [your feet as] winged [shoes]. Make the trip in one stage. Over the child [. . .] birds, *zariyanalla*-birds, [. . .] *arwanalla*-birds, eagles [. . .]. Let them . . . their pegs away from over him. [. . .] snakes intertwined [. . .]." [*The rest of column iii and the beginning of column iv lost.*]

§13 (iv 14–21) [. . .] seized [. . .] on the mound(?) [. . .] looked. [The . . . s . . .] bound(?). [. . .] on [that(?)] mound(?) [. . .] of love gives birth. [. . .] wherever [. . .].

§14 (iv 22–27) [A fisherman] said [to . . .]: "I will go see. [The . . . s] are standing in the mountains [. . . " The fisherman] arrived at the child. *zariyanalla*-birds [. . .] shelducks fly up. [. . .] are ascending(?) and they [. . .] to the sky.

§15 (iv 28–41) [When the fisherman approached], the poisonous snakes retired to a distance. [. . .] strokes (the child's) members along with its head. He strokes [. . .]. He strokes its eyes [. . .]. The fisherman said to himself: "Somehow I have pleased(?) the gods, so that they have removed the unfavorable bread from the rock.[2] I have struck the Sun God's fancy, and he has led me out (here) for the sake of [the child]. Do you perhaps know about me, O Sun God, that I have no child, that you have led me out (here) for the sake of the child? Truly the Sun God puts [. . .] bread out for him who is dear to him!" The fisherman lifted the child up from the ground, tidied him up, rejoiced in him, held him close to his chest, and carried him back home.

§16 (iv 42–52) The fisherman arrived at the city of Urma, went to his house, and sat down in a chair. The fisherman said to his wife: "Pay close attention to what I am about to say to you. Take this child, go into the bedroom, lie down on the bed, and wail. The whole city will hear and say: 'The fisherman's wife has borne a child!' And one will bring us bread, another will bring us beer, and still another will bring us fat. A(n ideal) woman's mind is clever. She has cut (herself) off from command(ing others). She is dependent(?) on the authority(?) of the god. She stands in woman's subordination(?), and she does not disobey (her) husband's word(?)."

§17 (iv 53–58) (The fisherman's wife) heard the man's word, went into [the bedroom], lay down on the bed, [and began to wail]. When the men of the city heard, they said: "[The fisherman's] wife [has borne a child!"] The men of the city [said this] and began to bring [things to her. One] brought [bread, and another] fat [and beer].

[*The colophon indicates that the story was continued on another tablet.*]

=========== **22. The Hunter Kessi and His Beautiful Wife** ===========

[*All of column i and the beginning of column ii are broken away.*]

§1 (A ii 1–3) [. . .] Kessi [. . . ed] the gods [. . .] became a hunter. [. . .] all the [. . .]s.

§2 (A ii 4–8) Kessi [took] in marriage the sister of Udubsarri, an evil(?) man. The woman's name was Sintalimeni. She was beautiful, endowed with everything. As a result Kessi had ears only for his wife. He no longer took account of the gods with thick loaves of bread and libations. Kessi no longer went into the mountains to hunt. He only had ears for his wife.

§3 (A ii 9–14) His mother said to Kessi: "Your wife alone has become your object of love. You don't go any more to the mountains to hunt. You don't bring me anything." Kessi took up (his) spear, called his little dogs behind him, and went to Mount Natara to hunt. But the gods were angry with Kessi because of the (neglected) libations. So they hid all the game from him.

§4 (A ii 15–19) Kessi roamed about in the mountains for three months, not wanting to go back to the city empty-handed, hungry and thirsty. A severe illness held Kessi for (those) three months. Kessi [. . . ed under] a tree [. . .] in the mountains the sons of the gods. . . . And [. . . ed] Kessi to eat [. . .]. Kessi's divine father [spoke(?)] down from the mountain:

§5 (A ii 20–23) "[. . .] you [*plural*] eat Kessi in the mountains [. . .], in/on his garment [. . .] lies. [. . .]."

[*The rest of column ii and the beginning of column iii are broken away.*]

§6 (A iii 2–3) (Kessi) saw [a second dream: . . .].

§7 (A iii 4–6) He saw [a third dream: . . .] brought [. . .] up from Mount Natara to the city of [. . .]. And [. . .]. And the servants went to his mother(?).

§8 (B ii 4–6) (He saw) a fourth dream: A heavy basalt boulder fell down from the sky and crushed the servants and the "man of god" under it.

§9 (B ii 7–8) He saw a fifth dream: Kessi's divine fathers were kindling a fire.

§10 (B ii 9–10) He saw a sixth dream: a wooden collar was lying on Kessi's neck, and below, a woman's anklet(?) had been placed on his (ankle).

§11 (B ii 11–13) He saw a seventh dream: Kessi went after lions. And as he ran out to the gate, he found serpents and sphinxes in front of the gate.

§12 (B ii 14–16) The next morning when the sun appeared in its radiance, Kessi arose from a sound sleep and began to describe the dreams of the night to his mother.

§13 (B ii 17–25) Kessi asked his mother: "How [shall we] act? Shall we go to the mountain? Shall we die in the mountain? Should [the . . . s] me in the mountains?" His mother replied to Kessi: "This is the meaning of the dreams: The grass grows tall. Dreams [. . .] of the city [. . .]. A river flows out from below it. [. . .] forest . . . in the day [. . .] we will [not(?)] die [. . .] blue wool [. . .]."

[*The rest of B ii is broken away. Portions of lines from column iii are preserved which are impossible to give in a connected translation. Preserved parts of still another tablet mention Kessi, a spear, going empty-handed to a city, heroes, and possibly dreams.*]

Notes

1. It appears that the Sun God copulated with the cow, since in the following context it gives birth to a two-legged being.

2. This saying in the language of fisherman probably means: "Now the fish will take my bait."

IV

A Canaanite Myth

23. Elkunirsa and Ashertu

The order of the fragments is that of Laroche (1969). The beginning of the tablet is broken off. As the text begins to be preserved, Elkunirsa's wife Ashertu is addressing Baal.

§1 (1 A i 1-7) ["Stay behind me, and I will stay] behind you. [Else I] will press [you] down with [my] word and stab [you] with [my] . . . I will move you [. . .]." Baal heard, stood [up], and went to the headwaters of the Euphrates River. He went [to] Elkunirsa, the husband of Ashertu, [and] entered the tent [of] Elkunirsa.

§2 (1 A i 8-21) Elkunirsa looked at Baal and asked him: "[Why] have you come?" Baal said: "When I came into your house, Ashertu sent young women to me, (saying:) 'Come sleep with me.' I refused. (Then) she . . . ed me [and] spoke [thus]: 'Stay behind me, [and] I will stay behind you. Else I will press you down with my [word] and [stab] you with my [. . .].' That is why I have come, my father. I did not come to you [in the person] of a messenger; I myself [have come] to you. Ashertu is rejecting you, her own[1] husband. [Although she is] your wife, yet she keeps sending to me: 'Sleep [with me].'" Elkunirsa [replied] to Baal: "Go threaten(?) her. [. . . Ashertu], my wife, and humble her."

§3 (1 A i 22-27) [Baal] heard the words of Elkunirsa and [went] to Ashertu. Baal said to Ashertu: "I have killed your seventy-seven [children]. (Your) eighty-eight I have killed." [When] Ashertu heard the humiliating report, her mind within her became sad. She appointed mourning [women]. And she lamented for seven years. [The . . . s] ate and drank for them. [*Break of undetermined length. When the text of the next fragment begins, Ashertu is speaking to her husband Elkunirsa.*]

§4 (2 B 1-3, 2 A ii 2-3) "[. . .] I will press [Baal] down [with my word. With] my [. . .] I will stab him. And I will sleep with you." [Elkunirsa] heard

69

and said to his wife: "Come [take] Baal as your [prisoner(?)], and do to him as you wish."

§5 (2 A ii 4-16) Anat-Astarte heard those words. She became a cup in Elkunirsa's hand. She became an owl(?) and perched on his wall. Anat-Astarte heard the words which husband and wife spoke to one another. Elkunirsa and his wife went to her bed and slept together. But Anat-Astarte flew off like a bird across the desert. In the desert she found Baal and said to him: "O Baal, [do not . . . the . . .] of Ashertu. Do not drink wine together. [Do not . . .] toward [. . .] is seeking [. . .]."

[*The tablet breaks here. Only a few signs of the following column are preserved. It would seem that Elkunirsa and Ashertu succeed in injuring Baal, for in the next fragment Baal is treated for injuries.*]

§6 (3 A iii 1-19) [. . .] dark [. . .] the gods his words [. . .] holds from the member. And to him [. . .] dark [. . .] the netherworld deities [. . .] up sleep. [The . . . s] . . . Anat-Astarte said (to?) the nether[world deities]: "If/When [. . . his] penis, tendons, muscles, [. . . . He(?) is] filthy with excrement. I will proceed to [. . .] (to?) you [*singular*]. [. . .] will become worse. Why have you sent[2] living persons to [the Dark] Earth?" [. . .] seized Baal's members, calves, like a snake. They [. . .]ed them [. . .]. Thus they said: "[. . .] his wife and children went [. . .], and they set up [. . .]." [. . .] began to say: "Do not [. . .] him. I will conduct [. . .] and [. . .] dark [. . .] and they will come(?)/see(?) [. . .]." [*The following context is broken away. The next fragment seems to describe Baal being exorcised.*]

§7 (4 A iii 1-6) [. . .] up [. . .] he went to Baal [. . .] Mother Goddesses to him [. . .] re-created [Baal. . . .] like a [. . . they] made him radiant[3].

§8 (4 A iii 7-11) The exorcists [. . .] to Baal. A man from Amurru, a man from Ana[. . .], chief of the . . . men. [They] exorcised him and [purified him] from oath, offense, [sin, evil] word [and . . .].

§9 (4 A iii 12-15) Baal's body [became pure. . . .] Anat-Astarte [said] to [. . . : "The . . . s have] re[created] Baal. [They have brought him back up] from the Dark [Earth." . . .] [*The text is broken away. The next fragment treats the same subject.*]

§10 (4 B iv 3-11) [. . .] if/when . . . to [. . .] I made. [. . .] the netherworld deities [. . .] Elkunirsa [. . .] brought. Anat-Astarte [. . .] conducted [. . .] appointed [. . .]. His/Her one child [. . .] (s)he made sleepy(?). [. . .]

§11 (4 B iv 12-19) [. . .] . . . [. . .] internal [. . . too from his head] a hair. He/She took sight from his [eyes]. He/She took hearing [from his ears]. He/She took . . . [from his. . . . He/She took] . . . from [his . . .] from his body [. . .]. [*The rest of the text is broken away.*]

Notes

1. The text erroneously has "your husband."
2. Or perhaps: "Why has he sent."
3. Or: "made him perfect"; cf. CHD sub *misriwahh-*.

Sources

In making these translations I have used published text editions or created my own editions based upon the arrangement of the sources in Laroche 1971 (abbreviated as CTH). For this reason it is unnecessary to list individual cuneiform texts used in creating the editions which underlie the translations in this book. In most cases, therefore, I only direct the interested reader to Laroche's CTH. In other cases I follow a particular published edition, e.g., Texts 16–18 and 21. Specific cuneiform texts are given in the bibliography only when there are very few which make up the text. The number of each entry corresponds to the number of the text translated in the main portion of the book.

1. CTH 321. **Editions:** Sayce 1922; Zimmern 1924; Beckman 1982.
   Transliterations: Friedrich 1967: 51–53; Laroche 1969: 5–12.
   Translations: Goetze 1957: 139–40; Zimmern 1922, idem in Goetze 1955: 125–126 (see H. G. Güterbock's comments in *Or* n.s. 20 [1951] 331–32); Gaster 1961: 245–67; Vieyra 1970: 526–29; Haas 1977: 109–14; Kühne 1978: 155–59; Bernabé 1987.
   Discussions: A sampling listed in Beckman 1982: 11. Additional discussions are Haas 1975; 1982: 45, 63–65; 1988a; Mora 1979.
2. CTH 324. **Transliterations:** Friedrich 1967: 53–55; Laroche 1969: 29–50.
   Translations: Goetze 1955: 126–28; Gaster 1961: 295–315; Vieyra 1970: 529–37; Moore 1975: 18–39; Haas 1977: 81–109; Kühne 1978: 159–65; Bernabé 1987: 47–59.
   Discussions: Otten 1942; Goetze 1957: 143–44; Kellerman 1986; 1987: esp. 113–14.
3. CTH 325. **Transliteration:** Laroche 1969: 52–59.
   Translations: Güterbock 1961: 144–48; DeVries 1967: 7–14; Moore 1975: 40–48; Bernabé 1987: 66–70.
   Discussion: Kellerman 1987: esp. 114–15.
4. CTH 671. **Edition:** Haas 1970: 140–74.
   Translation: Moore 1975: 217–20.
   Partial translation: Bernabé 1987: 88.
5a. CTH 326. **Transliteration:** Laroche 1969: 59–62.
   Translation: Moore 1975: 49–52.

5b. CTH 327. **Transliteration:** Laroche 1969: 62–64.
Translation: Moore 1975: 53–57.

6. CTH 322. **Transliteration:** Laroche 1969: 19–20.
Translation: DeVries 1967; Moore 1975: 161–63; Bernabé 1987: 79–81.
Discussion and translation of selected passages: Kellerman 1987: esp. 111–12.

7. CTH 323. **Transliteration:** Laroche 1969: 21–28.
Translations: Gurney 1961: 187–88; Gaster 1961: 270–94; DeVries 1967: 8ff. with notes on pp. 182ff.; Moore 1975: 164–79; Bernabé 1987: 61–64.
Discussion: Kellerman 1987: esp. 112–13; Yoshida forthcoming.

8. CTH 334. **Transliteration:** Laroche 1969: 78–86.
Translation: Moore 1975: 134–41.
Discussion: Kellerman 1987: esp. 116–18.

9. CTH 336. **Transliteration:** Laroche 1969: 87–96.
Translation: Moore 1975: 151–60.
Discussion: Kellerman 1987: esp. 118.

10. CTH 457.1. **Transliteration:** Laroche 1969: 106–8.
Discussion: del Monte 1979.

11. CTH 457.6. **Text:** KUB 43.60.
Translations: Moore 1975: 191–200; Calvert Watkins typescript in personal letter to the author. For the additional fragment, **Text:** KBo 22.178 (+) KUB 48.109 ii 2–11 (**Edition:** Hoffner 1988a).

12. CTH 727. **Text:** KUB 28.3–5.
Transliteration: Laroche 1969: 13–18.
Translation: Bossert 1946: 164–67; Goetze 1955: 120; Kammenhuber 1955: 113–14; Vieyra 1970: 525–26; Bernabé 1987: 75–77.

13. CTH 335. **Transliteration:** Laroche 1969: 97–105.

14. CTH 344. **Texts:** A = KUB 33.120 + 33.119 + 36.31; B = KUB 36.1 = A iii 26ff.
Transliterations: Güterbock 1946; Laroche; 1969: 153–61.
Translations: Forrer 1936; Güterbock 1946: 6–12; Otten 1950: 5–13; Goetze 1955: 120–21; Meriggi 1953: 110ff.; Vieyra 1970: 544–46; Kühne 1978: 153–55; Haas 1982: 131–34; Bernabé 1987: 146–55.
Discussions: Lesky 1950; Heubeck 1955; Steiner 1958; Walcot 1966: 1–26; Hoffner 1975: 138–39; Burkert 1979; Haas 1982: 133–48; Hoffner 1988b: 146–47, 165–66.

15. CTH 343. **Transliteration:** Laroche 1969:145–52.
Discussion and translation of excerpts: Güterbock 1961: 161–64; Bernabé 1987: 203–7.

16. CTH 364. **Edition:** Hoffner 1988b.
    Transliteration: Laroche 1969: 177–82.
    Translation: Bernabé 1987: 209–14.
    Discussion: Giorgadze 1988.
17. CTH 348. **Editions:** Friedrich 1949; Siegelová 1971: 35–87.
    Transliteration: Laroche 1969: 169–76.
    Translation: Bernabé 1987: 160–70.
    Discussion: Haas 1982: 120–21.
18. CTH 345. **Editions:** Güterbock 1946, 1952.
    Translations: Goetze 1955: 121–25; Vieyra 1970: 546–54; Kühne 1978: 151–52; Haas 1982: 149–60; Bernabé 1987: 171–99.
    Discussion: Komoróczy 1973.
19. CTH 7.1. **Edition:** Otten 1973.
    Translation: Haas 1977: 14–17.
    Discussion: Hoffner 1980: 289–91.
20. CTH 360. **Editions:** Friedrich 1950; Siegelová 1971.
    Translation: Bernabé 1987: 217–28. In my translation the column numbers and line count given after the § numbers are based on the cumulative column and line count in Siegelová 1971. I denote the first long reconstructed fragment in her edition here as "1," although it is reconstructed from Siegelová's texts 1–10.
21. CTH 363. **Edition:** Güterbock 1946; Friedrich 1950.
    Discussion: Hoffner 1981.
22. CTH 361. **Edition:** Friedrich 1950. Portions of a unilingual Hurrian story of Kessi are also known, but no translation of them has been produced.
23. CTH 342. **Edition:** Otten 1953.
    Transliteration: Laroche 1969: 139–44.
    Translation and discussion: Hoffner 1965.
    Translation: Goetze 1955: 519–20. The text sigla in the translation follow Laroche 1969: 139–44.

Concordance

Bibliography

Archi, A.
1982   "I Poteri della dea Istar Hurrita-Ittita." *OA* 16: 298–311.

Astour, M.
1989   *Hittite History and Absolute Chronology of the Bronze Age.* Studies in Mediterranean Archaeology and Literature 73. Gothenburg. Sweden: Paul Åströms Förlag.

Beckman, G.
1982   "The Anatolian Myth of Illuyanka." *JANES* 14: 11–25.
1986   "Proverbs and Proverbial Allusions in Hittite." *JNES* 45: 19–30.

Bernabé, A.
1987   *Textos literarios hetitas.* Madrid: Alianza Editorial.

Bossert, H.
1946   *Asia.* Istanbul: Literarische Fakultät der Universität.

Burkert, W.
1979   "Von Ullikummi zum Kaukasus: Die Felsgeburt des Unholds. Zur Kontinuität einer mündlichen Erzählung." *Würzburger Jahrbücher für die Altertumswissenschaft* NF 5: 253–61.

Cornil, P.
1988   "Les Mythes de l'Asie Mineure au 2e Millénaire avant J.-C., Temps mythique et temps historique dans les traditions anciennes." *Ludus Magistralis* 21: 7–12.

Deighton, H. J.
1982   *The Weather-God in Hittite Anatolia: An examination of the archaeological and textual sources.* Oxford: B.A.R.

del Monte, G. F.
1979   "Il mitologema de *Kataḫziwuri*." Pp. 109–20 in *Studia Mediterranea Piero Meriggi dicata.* Ed. by O. Carruba. Pavia: Aurora Edizioni.

del Monte, G. F., and J. Tischler
1978   *Die Orts- und Gewässernamen der hethitischen Texte.* Répertoire Géographique des Textes Cunéiformes. Wiesbaden: Dr. Ludwig Reichert Verlag.

DeVries, B.
1967   *The Style of Hittite Epic and Mythology.* Ann Arbor: University Microfilms.

Dirlmeier, F.
1955   "Homerisches Epos und Orient." *RhM* 98: 18–37.

Forrer, E.
1936   "Eine Geschichte des Götterkönigtums aus dem Hatti-Reiche." *Annuaire de l'institut de philologie et d'histoire orientales* 4: 687–713.

Friedrich, J.
1949   "Der churritische Mythus vom Schlangendämon Hedammu in hethitischer Sprache." *ArOr* 17: 230–54.
1950   "Churritische Märchen und Sagen in hethitischer Sprache." *ZA* 49: 213–54.
1967   *Hethitisches Elementarbuch. Zweiter Teil. Lesestücke in Transkription mit Erläuterungen und Wörterverzeichnissen.* Heidelberg: Carl Winter Universitätsverlag.

Gaster, T. H.
1961   *Thespis: Ritual, Myth, and Drama in the Ancient Near East.* Garden City, NY: Doubleday.

Giorgadze, G.
1988   "On the Word for 'Silver' with Reference to Hittite Cuneiform Texts." *AoF* 15: 69–75.

Goetze, A.
1955   "Hittite Myths, Epics, and Legends." Pp. 120–28 in *Ancient Near Eastern Texts Relating to the Old Testament.* Ed. by J. B. Pritchard. Princeton, NJ: Princeton University Press.
1957   *Kleinasien.* Handbuch der Altertumswissenschaft. Kulturgeschichte des Alten Orients. Munich: Beck.

Gurney, O. R.
1958   "Hittite Kingship." Pp. 105–21 in *Myth, Ritual and Kingship.* Ed. by S. H. Hooke. Oxford: Clarendon Press.
1961   *The Hittites.* Baltimore: Penguin Books.

Güterbock, H. G.
1934   "Die historische Tradition und ihre literarische Gestaltung bei Babyloniern und Hethitern bis 1200 (1. Teil)." *ZA* 42: 1–91.
1936   "Die historische Tradition und ihre literarische Gestaltung bei Babyloniern und Hethitern bis 1200 (2. Teil)." *ZA* 44: 45–149.
1946   *Kumarbi: Mythen vom churritischen Kronos.* Zurich: Europa Verlag.
1948   "The Hittite Version of the Hurrian Kumarbi Myths: Oriental Forerunners to Hesiod." *AJA* 52: 123–34.
1952   *The Song of Ullikummi: Revised Text of the Hittite Version of a Hurrian Myth.* New Haven: American Schools of Oriental Research.

1961   "Hittite Mythology." Pp. 139–79 in *Mythologies of the Ancient World*. Ed. S. N. Kramer. Garden City, NY: Doubleday.

1978   "Mythen, Epen und Erzählungen." Pp. 232–49 in *Neues Handbuch der Literatur-Wissenschaft*. Ed. W. Röllig. Wiesbaden: Athenaion.

1983   "Hittite Historiography: A Survey." Pp. 21–35 in *History, Historiography and Interpretation: Studies in Biblical and Cuneiform Literatures*. Ed. by H. Tadmor and M. Weinfeld. Jerusalem: Magnes Press, Hebrew University.

Haas, V.

1970   *Der Kult von Nerik*. Studia Pohl. Dissertationes Scientificae de Rebus Orientis Antiqui 4. Rome: Pontificium Institutum Biblicum.

1975   "Jason's Raub des goldenen Vliesses im Lichte hethitischer Quellen." *UF* 7: 227–33.

1977   *Magie und Mythen im Reich der Hethiter: I. Vegetationskulte und Pflanzenmagie*. Hamburg: Merlin Verlag.

1980   "Betrachtungen zum ursprunglichen Schauplatz der Mythen vom Gott Kumarbi." *SMEA* 22: 97–105.

1982   *Hethitische Berggötter und hurritische Steindämonen: Riten, Kulte und Mythen. Eine Einführung in die altkleinasiatischen religiösen Vorstellungen*. Kulturgeschichte der Antiken Welt. Mainz am Rhein: Verlag Philipp von Zabern.

1988a   "Betrachtungen zur Rekonstruktion des hethitischen Frühjahrsfestes (EZEN purulliyas)." *ZA* 78: 284–98.

1988b   "Magie in hethitischen Gärten." Pp. 121–42 in *Documentum Asiae Minoris Antiquae*. Ed. by E. Neu and C. Rüster. Wiesbaden: Harrassowitz.

Hecker, K.

1977   "Tradition und Originalität in der altorientalischen Literatur." *ArOr* 45: 245–58.

Heubeck, A.

1955   "Mythologische Vorstellungen des Alten Orients im archäischen Griechentum." *Gymnasium* 62: 508–25.

Hoffner, H. A., Jr.

1965   "The Elkunirša Myth Reconsidered." *RHA* 23: 5–16.

1975   "Hittite Mythological Texts: A Survey." Pp. 136–45 in *Unity and Diversity: Essays in the History, Literature, and Religion of the Ancient Near East*. Ed. by H. Goedicke and J. J. M. Roberts. Baltimore: The Johns Hopkins University Press.

1980   "Histories and Historians of the Ancient Near East: The Hittites." *Or* 49: 283–332.

1981   "The Hurrian Story of the Sungod, the Cow and the Fisherman." Pp. 189–94 in *Studies on the Civilization and Culture of Nuzi and the Hurrians in Honor of E. R. Lacheman*. Ed. by M. Morrison and D. I. Owen. Winona Lake, IN: Eisenbrauns.

1988a   "A Scene in the Realm of the Dead." Pp. 191–99 in *A Scientific Humanist: Studies in Memory of Abraham Sachs*. Ed. by E. Leichty, M. d. Ellis and P. Gerardi. Philadelphia: University Museum.

1988b   "The Song of Silver." Pp. 143–66 in *Documentum Asiae Minoris Antiquae*. Ed. by E. Neu and C. Rüster. Wiesbaden: Harrassowitz.

Imparati, F.
1979   "Il culto della dea Ningal presso gli ittiti." Pp. 293–324 in *Studia Mediterranea Piero Meriggi dicata*. Ed. by O. Carruba. Pavia: Aurora Edizioni.

Jakob-Rost, L.
1977   *Das Lied von Ullikummi: Dichtungen der Hethiter*. Leipzig: Insel Verlag.

Kammenhuber, A.
1955   "Die protohattisch-hethitische Bilinguis vom Mond, der vom Himmel gefallen ist." *ZA* 55: 102–23.

Kellerman, G.
1986   "The Telepinu Myth Reconsidered." Pp. 115–24 in *Kaniššuwar*. Ed. by H. A. Hoffner, Jr., and G. Beckman. Chicago: Oriental Institute.

1987   "La déesse Hannahanna: son image et sa place dans les mythes anatoliens." *Hethitica* 7: 109–48.

Kirk, G. S.
1970   *Myth: Its Meaning and Functions in Ancient and Other Cultures*. Berkeley: University of California Press.

Klengel, H.
1988   "Die Keilschrifttexte von Meskene und die Geschichte von Astata/Emar." *OLZ* 83: 645–53.

Komoróczy, G.
1973   "'The Separation of Sky and Earth': The Cycle of Kumarbi and the Myths of Cosmogony in Mesopotamia." *Acta Antiqua* 21: 21–45.

Kühne, C.
1978   "Hittite Texts." Pp. 146–84 in *Near Eastern Religious Texts Relating to the Old Testament*. Ed. by W. Beyerlin. Philadelphia: Westminster.

Laroche, E.
1969   *Textes mythologiques hittites en transcription*. Paris: Klincksieck.
1971   *Catalogue des textes hittites*. Études et Commentaires. Paris: Klincksieck.
1976   "Panthéon national et panthéons locaux chez les Hourrites." *Or* 45: 94–99.

1988   "Observations sur le rituel anatolien provenant de Meskene-Emar." Pp. 111–17 in *Studi di Storia e di Filologia Anatolica dedicati a Giovanni Pugliese Carratelli.* Ed. by F. Imparati. Florence: Edizioni Librarie Italiane Estere.

Lesky, A.
1950   "Hethitische Texte und griechischer Mythos." *Anzeiger der Österreichischen Akademie der Wissenschaften. Philosophisch-historische Klasse* 87: 137–60.

Macqueen, J.
1959   "Hattian Mythology and Hittite Monarchy." *AnSt* 9: 171–88.

McMahon, J. G.
1988   "The Hittite State Cult of the Tutelary Deities." Ph.D. diss., The University of Chicago.

Meriggi, P.
1953   "I Miti di Kumarpi, il Kronos Currico." *Studi Periodici di Letteratura e Storia dell'Antichità* 31: 101–57.

Miller, P.
1980   "El, the Creator of Earth." *BASOR* 239: 43–46.

Moore, G. C.
1975   "The Disappearing Deity Motif in Hittite Texts." BLitt. thesis, Oxford.

Mora, C.
1979   "Sulla mitologia ittita di origine anatolica." Pp. 373–85 in *Studia Mediterranea Piero Meriggi dicata.* Ed. by O. Carruba. Pavia: Aurora Edizioni.

Neu, E.
1988a   *Das Hurritische: Eine altorientalische Sprache in neuem Licht.* Akademie der Wissenschaften und der Literatur, Abhandlungen der Geistes- und Sozialwissenschaftlichen Klasse. Stuttgart: Franz Steiner.

1988b   "Varia Hurritica: Sprachliche Beobachtungen an der hurritisch-hethitischen Bilingue aus Hattusa." Pp. 235–54 in *Documentum Asiae Minoris Antiquae.* Ed. by E. Neu and C. Rüster. Wiesbaden: Harrassowitz.

1988c   "Zur Grammatik des Hurritischen auf der Grundlage der hurritisch-hethitischen Bilingue aus der Boğazköy-Grabungskampagne 1983." Pp. 95–115 in *Hurriter und Hurritisch.* Ed. by V. Haas. Konstanz: Universitätsverlag Konstanz.

1989   "Neue Wege im Hurritischen." Pp. 293–303 in *ZDMG Suppl.* 7.

Otten, H.
1942   *Die Überlieferung des Telipinu-Mythus.* Leipzig: Vorderasiatisch-Aegyptische Gesellschaft.

1950   *Mythen vom Gotte Kumarbi: Neue Fragmente.* Deutsche Akademie der Wissenschaften zu Berlin, Institut für Orientforschung. Berlin: Akademie-Verlag.

1953   "Ein kanaanäischer Mythus aus Bogazköy." *MIO* 1: 125–50.

1973   *Eine althethitische Erzählung um die Stadt Zalpa.* Studien zu den Boğazköy-Texten, Heft 17. Wiesbaden: Harrassowitz.

1984a   "Blick in die altorientalische Geisteswelt: Neufund einer hethitischen Tempelbibliothek." Pp. 50–60 in *Jahrbuch der Akademie der Wissenschaften in Göttingen.*

1984b   "Die Tontafelfunde aus Haus 16." *AA* 372–75.

1986   "Ebla in der hurritisch-hethitischen Bilingue aus Boğazköy." Paper presented at symposium, Wirtschaft und Gesellschaft in Ebla, at Heidelberg.

Owen, D. I., and R. Veenker
1987   "Megum, the First Ur III Ensi of Ebla." Pp. 263–91 and Plates I–II in *Ebla 1975–1985: Dieci anni di studi linguistici e filologici.* Ed. by L. Cagni. Napoli: Istituto Universitario Orientale. Dipartimento di studi asiatici.

Pecchioli Daddi, F.
1987   "Aspects du culte de la divinité hattie Teteshapi." Pp. 361–80 in *Hethitica VIII: Acta Anatolica E. Laroche oblata.* Ed. by R. Lebrun. Louvain and Paris: Peeters.

Pecchioli Daddi, F., and A. M. Polvani
        "Miti e racconti degli Ittiti." *Paideia* (forthcoming).

Salvini, M.
1977   "Sui testi mitologici in lingua hurrita." *SMEA* 18: 73–91.

Sandars, N. K.
1980   "The Sea Peoples." *AJA* 60: 366–69.

Sayce, A.
1922   "Hittite Legend of the War with the Great Serpent." *JRAS* 177–90.

Siegelová, J.
1971   *Appu-Märchen und Hedammu-Mythus.* Studien zu den Bogazköy-Texten 14. Wiesbaden: Harrassowitz.

Singer, I.
1988   "The Origin of the Sea Peoples and their Settlement on the Coast of Canaan." Pp. 239–50 in *Society and Economy in the Eastern Mediterranean (c. 1500–1000 B.C.).* Ed. by M. Heltzer and E. Lipinski. Leuven: Peeters.

Soysal, O.
1988   "Einige Überlegungen zu KBo III 60." *VO* 7: 107–28.

Steiner, G.
1958   "Der Sukzessionsmythos in Hesiods 'Theogony' und ihren orientalischen Parallelen." Ph.D. diss., Universität Hamburg.

Vieyra, M.
1970   "Les textes hittites." Pp. 459–566 in *Les religions du Proche-Orient asiatique.* Paris: Fayard/Denoel.
von Schuler, E.
1965   "Kleinasien: Die Mythologie der Hethiter und Hurriter." Pp. 141–215 in *Wörterbuch der Mythologie.* Ed. by H. W. Haussig. Stuttgart: Ernst Klett Verlag.
Walcot, P.
1966   *Hesiod and the Near East.* Cardiff: University of Wales Press.
Wilhelm, G., and J. Boese
1987   "Absolute Chronologie und die hethitische Geschichte des 15. und 14. Jahrhunderts v. Chr." Pp. 74–117 in *High, Middle or Low? Acts of an International Colloquium on Absolute Chronology Held at the University of Gothenburg 20th–22nd August 1987. Part 1.* Ed. by P. Åström. Gothenburg, Sweden: Paul Åströms Förlag.
Yoshida, D.
           "Die Sonnengottheiten bei den Hethitern." Ph.D. diss., Munich (forthcoming).
Zimmern, H.
1922   Pp. 339–40 in *Textbuch zur Religionsgeschichte.* Ed. by E. Lehmann and H. Haas. Leipzig: A. Deichert.
1924   "Der Kampf des Wettergottes mit der Schlange Illujankaš." Pp. 430–41 in *Stand und Aufgaben der Sprachwissenschaft: Festschrift für Wilhelm Streitberg.* Ed. by J. Friedrich, J. B. Hofmann and W. Horn. Heidelberg: Carl Winter Universitätsverlag.

Glossary

Alalu Mesopotamian god who in the Kumarbi myths appears as the first king of the gods and father of Kumarbi. See Text 14.

AMMATU Unit of linear measure (= *gipessar*, probably 0.5 m.) equal to 1/30 of an IKU (probably 15 m.) or 1/3,000 of a DANNA (probably 1.5 km.).

Anat-Astarte The sister of the god Baal, who seeks to protect him against the evil plots of the goddess Asherah.

Anu Mesopotamian sky god, who in the Hurro-Hittite Kumarbi myths appears as the second king of the gods and the father of Tessub and his brothers.

ANUNNAKI A very important group of gods, who in the Hurro-Hittite conception presently dwell in the netherworld. The term is a Sumerogram, which probably corresponds to Hittite "primeval gods" (*karuiles siunes*).

Apzuwa What in the Hittite Kumarbi myths is written as a city name is a transformation of an old Sumerian name for the subterranean sweet waters, the home of the god Enki-Ea.

Arinna The home of the cult of a Sun Goddess, who was the principal female deity in the Hittite pantheon. This Sun Goddess was eventually equated with the Hurrian goddess Hebat.

arkammi A musical instrument, paired with the *galgalturi*.

Asherah Wife of the West Semitic god El (or Elkunirsa). See Text 23.

Asmunikal The queen of King Arnuwanda I, successor and son-in-law of Tudhaliya II.

Astabi See ZABABA.

Baal Epithet of the West Semitic god Haddu. See Text 23.

BALAG(.DI) A stringed instrument.

Basalt A common epithet for the stone monster Ullikummi.

DANNA Roughly a mile. See *AMMATU.*

Dark Earth A term for the netherworld.

Ea Mesopotamian god of the subterranean sweet waters, lord or king of wisdom. Also known there as Enki.

Earth Hittite Daganzipas, personified as a goddess in Text 14.

Elkunirsa The Hittite spelling of the West Semitic divine name "El, the Creator of Earth." He was the husband of the goddess Asherah (= Ashertu) and lived in a tent at the headwaters of the Euphrates (= Mala) River.

eyan-tree An evergreen tree which served as a religious symbol. An *eyan-tree* was planted in front of the homes of persons exempted from certain public obligations, such as corvée work or taxes.

Frost Tentative translation of *hahhimas* which designates a powerful personified force in Text 7. Since he appears after the sun disappears and his effect on gods and nature is to paralyze them, it seems likely that he is a manifestation of cold.

galaktar A plant product highly esteemed to produce tranquillity. The mode of consumption is never specified, whether eating or sniffing. Some think it was a drug.

galgalturi A percussion instrument.

GUDU An official in the cult. The Sumerian term meant "anointed," but we have no evidence that the Hittites so understood it. In small temples he formed together with the SANGA ("priest") and the AMA DINGIR-LIM ("mother of the god") the minimal staff. See Text 1.

halenzu A plant which grew in the moor and could be found on the surface of lakes and ponds.

handatar A word that can denote a god's power to control the course of events. See Text 16, § 1.1.

Hannahanna A Mother Goddess whose advice is regularly sought by other gods in the Old Hittite Vanishing God Myths. Her name appears to be a reduplicated form of the Hittite word "grandmother."

Hapantali A Hattian god who figures in Old Hittite myths.

hapupi-bird A bird of the steppes and wilderness areas, possibly an owl.

Hebat Hurrian goddess, consort of Tessub. Queen of the gods. Equated by the Hittites with the Sun Goddess of Arinna.

Hedammu A huge male sea monster which terrorizes gods and men in Text 17. He is probably the child of Kumarbi and Sertapsuruhi, the daughter of the Sea God.

hunting bag An important religious symbol which figures in the Old Hittite Vanishing God Myths. In festival descriptions the hunting bag (Hittite *kursas*) represented the god LAMMA and served as a focus of his worship.

Hupasiya A man from the town of Ziggaratta who plays a role in the Illuyanka myth.

IKU See *AMMATU.*

Illuyanka A Hattian or Hittite common noun meaning "serpent" used as the designation of the foe of the Storm God in the Illuyanka Myth.

Impaluri The vizier of the Sea God in the Hurro-Hittite Kumarbi myths.

Inara   A goddess, a daughter of the great Storm God, who seems to have roamed the steppe, perhaps as a huntress. She figures in Old Hittite myths with a Hattian background.

Irsirras   A group of deities who at the bidding of Kumarbi, carry Ulli-kummi secretly to the netherworld after his birth.

ISHTAR instruments   Stringed instruments similar to lyres. Large and small varieties are mentioned in texts and depicted in art. The large variety is so big it must be carried by two grown men.

Izzummi   Vizier of the god Ea.

Kamrusepa   A goddess of magic. Her Hattian name was Kattahziwuri.

Kanzura   A divine mountain who is born from Anu's seed which impregnated Kumarbi. A brother of Tessub.

Kattahziwuri   See Kamrusepa.

Kubaba   Goddess attested already in Anatolia of the pre-Old Hittite period, but integral to the Hurrian pantheon. Her chief cult center was Carchemish.

KUKUBU   A vessel of unknown capacity, used to contain fluids.

Kumarbi   A grain deity, equated with Semitic Dagan in god lists from Ugarit. Son of the god Alalu. Third king of the gods. Called "wise king" and "Father of the Gods." His chief cult center was the North Mesopotamian city of Urkis. Chief antagonist of Tessub in the cycle of Kumarbi myths. Couples sexually with various females, including a wife, Sertapsuruhi the daughter of the Sea God, and becomes the father of many gods and monsters (Ullikummi, Hedammu, Silver, and possibly LAMMA).

Kummiya   The home of the god Tessub, located in Northern Syria.

kuntarra-shrine   The holiest of holies of the chief god Tessub. Located in heaven in Text 18, but mentioned in a Hittite treaty as a real building in the Anatolian city of Tarhuntassa.

LAMMA   A Hurrian male deity, whom the god Kumarbi and Ea for a time made king of the gods.

liti   An oil-yielding plant.

mal   A quality prized in warriors.

Mukisanu   The vizier and messenger of Kumarbi.

Nara Napsara   Although written as two divine names in succession, this combination denotes a single netherworld god, the brother of the god Ea. Occasionally the name is written simply Nara.

Nerik   A city in north central Asia Minor along the lower course of the Marassanta River (=Turkish Kızılırmak). It was a major cult center for the Storm God, which was cut off from Hittite control for many years and recovered by Hattusili III.

palhi-vessel   A large, wide-mouthed pot having a lid, and occasionally made of bronze. Used to contain beverages and to store grain.

parhuenas   A sweet plant.

Purulli A Hittite festival celebrated in the spring. See Text 1.

Sauska Bellicose and beautiful sister of the god Tessub. Functionally similar to the West Semitic goddess Anat-Astarte, sister of Baal. Written *ISHTAR* in the texts, often specifically *ISHTAR* of Nineveh.

Sea God In the Old Hittite myths he appears as the kidnapper of the Sun God and the father of the wife of Telipinu. In the New Hittite Kumarbi myths he is allied with Kumarbi, to whom he gives his daughter Sertap-suruhi in marriage.

Seri and Hurri The divine bulls who draw Tessub's cart.

Sun God In Old Hittite myths he is the Hattian solar deity Estan, son of the Great Storm God and brother of Telipinu. In New Hittite Kumarbi myths he is the Hurrian solar deity Simige, an ally of Tessub.

Sun Goddess of Arinna The chief goddess in the New Hittite pantheon, whose consort was the great Storm God. In the New Kingdom they were identified with Hebat and Tessub.

Sun Goddess of the Earth (= nether world) Her name in Old Hittite, Hattian contexts is unknown. In New Hittite texts with a Hurrian background she is referred to either by the descriptive title "Sun Deity of the Earth" or by the Hurrian word Allani "the lady."

Suwaliyat See Tasmisu.

Tabarna Originally a personal name, this term came to be a title or designation of all Hittite emperors. The practice is similar to the Roman use of Caesar.

Takiti Maidservant of the goddess Hebat.

Tasmisu Hurrian name of the brother and vizier of Tessub, antagonist of Kumarbi. His Hittite name was Suwaliyat.

Tawannanna Originally the name of a Hittite queen, this term came to be a title or designation of all Hittite queens. See Tabarna.

Telipinu A Storm God, son of the great Storm God, whose anger and disappearance form the subject of several Old Hittite myths. Like other Storm Gods, Telipinu gave success to agricultural activities such as plowing, sowing seed, and harvesting.

tenawas An evil force, sometimes portrayed topographically, which seizes souls in the afterlife, causing forgetfulness. It may be compared to Lethe, the mythological Greek River of Forgetfulness.

Tessub The supreme Storm God. Reigning king of the gods according to Hurrian theology. Son of Anu. His consort is Hebat (= Sun Goddess of Arinna). His sons are Sarruma and the Storm God of Nerik. His vizier is Tasmi(su). His two divine bulls are Seri(su) and Hurri (or Tella). His principal cult center and "home" is Kummiya in Northern Mesopotamia.

Thousand Gods A standard way of referring to the entire pantheon.

Tutelary Deity   (Sumerian LAMMA). A type of deity whose function is to protect either an individual worshiper or some aspect of the physical world.

Ubelluri   A Hurrian god like the Greek Atlas, who dwells in the netherworld and holds up heaven and earth.

Ullikummi   Blind and deaf stone monster which Kumarbi engenders from sexual union with a huge boulder or cliff.

War God   See ZABABA.

Wurunkatte   See ZABABA.

ZABABA   Sumerogram denoting the Hittite War God. His Hattian name was Wurunkatte ("king of the land"). In the Kumarbi myths he seems to be Astabi, an ally of Tessub.

Zaliyanu   A deified mountain near the city of Nerik.

Indexes

Persons

Appu (m.), 63
Ashapa (m.), 43
Asmunikal (f.), 24
Hupasiya (m.), 11, 12
Kella (m.), 11, 13, 14
LAMMA.SUM (m.), 43
Pihaziti (m.), 14
Right (m.), 64

Sintalimeni (f.), 67
Tahpurili (m.), 13
Udubsarri (m.), 67
Walwaziti, the chief scribe
  (m.), 14
Warsiya (m.), 43
Wrong (m.), 64
Zita (m.), 43

Deities

A.GILIM (m.), 41
Alalu (m.), 40
Ammezzadu (m.), 40
Ammunki (f.), 40
Anu (m.), 40, 41, 42
Astabi (m.), 57
Atlas (m.), *see* Ubelluri

Dark Earth (f.), 15, 16, 17, 22, 28, 32, 40
Dark Goddess, 16

Ea (m.), 39, 41, 42, 43, 49
Earth Goddess, 43
Ellil (m.), 40, 41, 55, 59
ERESHKIGAL (f.), 22

Fate Goddesses, 16, 36, 42, 53, 54

Frost (m.), 14, 27

Gulsa (f.), 21, 27

Hannahanna (f.), 15, 18, 21, 26, 27, 28, 29, 30
Hapantali (m.), 16, 29, 34
Hasamili (m.), 27
Hebat (f.), 57
Heptad of the Storm God, 35

Impaluri (m.), 53
Inara (f.), 11, 12, 30
Irsirra deities (f.), 54
Ishara (f.), 40
Istustaya (f.), 16
Izzummi (m.), 44

KA.ZAL (m.), 41
Kamrusepa (f.), 16, 32, 34

87

Places

General